Praise for *An Abundant Life Beyond Retirement*

'Sadly, too many people do not plan for when they leave full-time employment – what we call retirement. I like to think that we all never really retire from work – we just have different stages in our lives where we work at different things. Like all changes in life, we all need to think and plan about what is important, what we want to do and achieve, and the contributions we want to make. Peter Cheel has written an excellent book to help us think about these changes in a simple and structured way – to help us live our lives with purpose. I would highly recommend this book to you and hope it helps you to realise your ambitions, brings you fulfilment and wellbeing.'

—David Thodey AO, FTSE, ATSE – Chancellor of the University of Sydney and Chair of Ramsay and Xero

'As retirement approaches, there is much more than finances to consider, and this book provides words of wisdom and action. Grounded in years of research and observations, this is a must-read for those who want to make the most of life in retirement.'

—Professor Marian Baird AO, FASSA – Professor of Gender and Employment Relations and Head of the Discipline of Work and Organisational Studies, University of Sydney

'In *An Abundant Life Beyond Retirement*, Peter Cheel reminds us that retirement is not the "end," but the time for change in how we work and live. He speaks with hope and clarity to those entering this new season of life, helping them navigate change with purpose, generosity, and faithfulness. It is a wise and practical guide for anyone looking to discern how their gifts and skills can continue to serve others.'

—The Right Reverend Chris Edwards – Bishop of Northern Region in the Anglican Diocese of Sydney

'Moving into retirement post full-time work is an important phase, perhaps the most significant life transition in the decades since we entered the workforce. It is a time filled with both challenges and opportunities. It needs to be navigated with purpose, intention and with some assistance from a retirement coach. This book provides a comprehensive outline of the major topics to consider and many very useful tools and resources. I look forward to using this book personally and believe many others will benefit from it as well.'

—Andrew Thorburn – Chief Executive Officer, Hammond Care

'This book offered me clear, practical guidance on thriving in retirement. It moves beyond finances to address purpose, identity, and joy and instils confidence in the reader. It is an essential read for anyone considering the transition.'

—Catherine Fritz-Kalish AM – Co-Founder & Managing Director, Global Access Partners

AN ABUNDANT LIFE BEYOND RETIREMENT

How to Plan and Live with Purpose

PETER A. CHEEL

An Abundant Life Beyond Retirement
How to Plan and Live with Purpose

Peter A. Cheel

First edition: March 2026

ISBN 978-0-9925430-1-3

 A catalogue record for this publication is available from the National Library of Australia.

Jacket Cover Design: Julia Kuris

Page design and typesetting: Michelle Pirovich

Printed by: Ingram Spark

Contact the Author: peteracheel@gmail.com

DISCLAIMER: This book is for informational purposes only and does not constitute financial, legal, or investment advice. Readers should consult qualified professionals before making any financial/non-financial decisions.

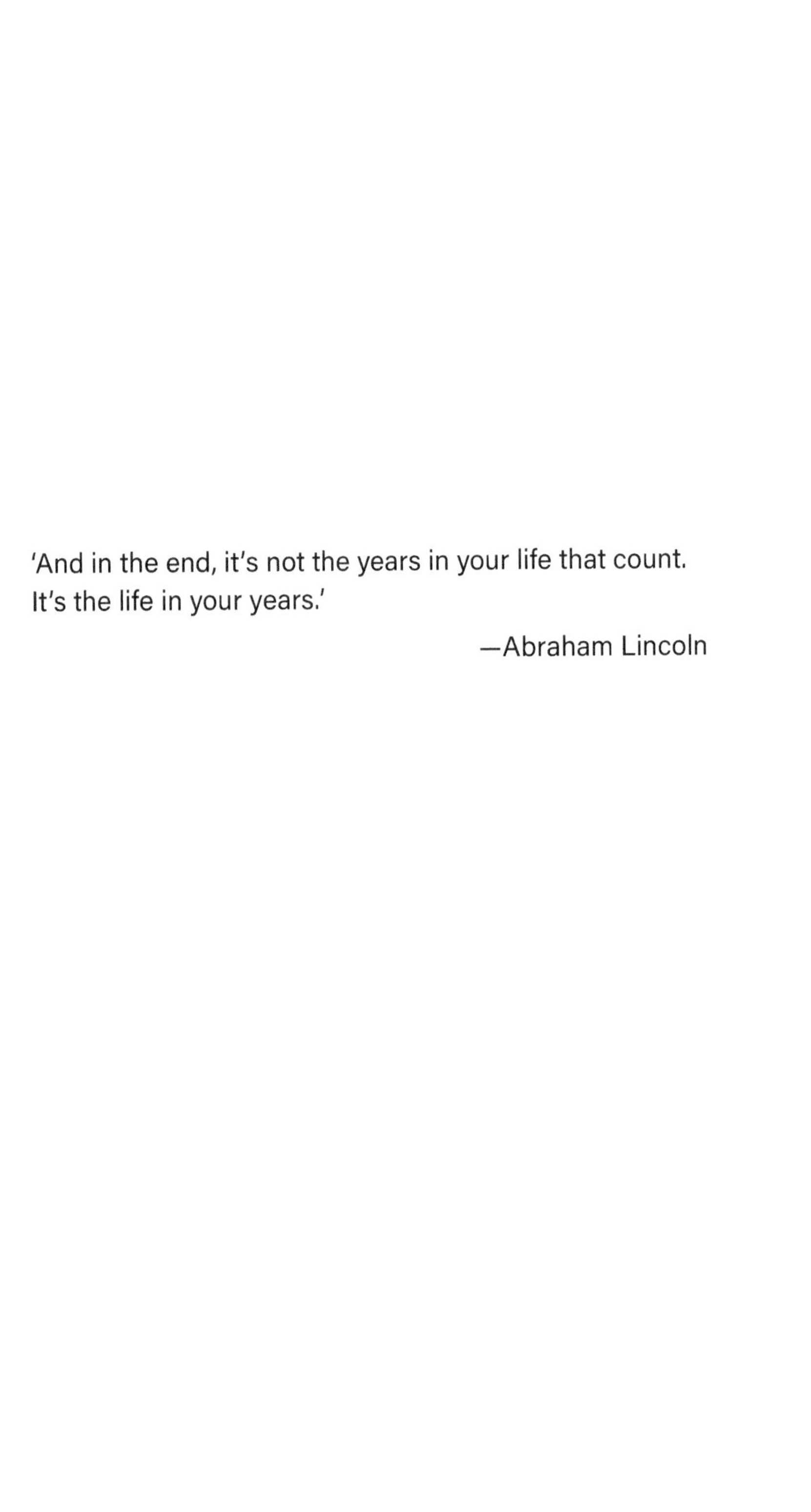

'And in the end, it's not the years in your life that count.
It's the life in your years.'

—Abraham Lincoln

This book is dedicated to Clair, Thomas and Chloe...
you mean the world to me!

CONTENTS

FOREWORD

Thinking carefully and widely about the way we conduct every stage of our lives is a very desirable thing to do, and retirement from our full-time, main career is no exception.

The concept of retirement means many things to many people, and has changed very significantly as well over the years, but we all assume that at some point in our lives we will need to transition away from the primary income-earning activities that have been our lot in our working lives.

Germany, under Chancellor Otto von Bismarck, was the first nation to introduce old age pensions in 1889. Eligibility began at age 70, but very few people – perhaps only one in nine – accessed it because life spans were so much shorter.

Here in Australia, State governments started introducing pensions from around 1900, and the newly-created Commonwealth government first introduced a national scheme in 1908. It was modest and non-contributory, providing around 26 pounds per year for men from age 65 and women from age 60, and was subject to a strict means test and the demonstration of good character!

For many decades this broad model remained in place, but was to undergo a transformation from 1992 with the introduction of a mandatory superannuation scheme which has increased hugely over time and which, though it operates alongside the pension scheme, now provides retirement income for around 27% of retirees, a number which will rise strongly in coming years. In fact a staggering

$4 billion are invested in Australian super funds, which is equivalent to around 150% of the country's annual GDP.

There is no doubt that these arrangements increasingly underpin the other enormous changes in the way in which people both plan for, and undertake, retirement.

Australians now live much longer, and remain much healthier and active than in the past as medicine, diets and safety have advanced under (and at the same time accelerated) our increased prosperity. Furthermore, the changing nature of work means that the wearing out of the body through sheer hard labour is less the norm than in times gone by. Many of us can remain working full or part-time than was the case in the past.

And so now, many Australians think of retirement from the workplace at 65 or so for men and 60 for women as an outdated model. Increasingly Australians are moving to more flexible and gradual transitions that often involve working longer. The 'stop work at 65' model is fading, and indeed given the very real economic and cultural challenges of an ageing demographic this trend is likely to be encouraged by Governments seeking to retain as many taxpayers as possible for as long as possible in the future.

Enter a most useful resource: this book, *An Abundant Life Beyond Retirement*, by Peter Cheel.

It fully recognises the great changes in retirement arrangements that are upon us, and provides a truly useful guide to help people think through their retirements – typically, Australians start to ponder the issue in their late 40s – and furthermore provide very helpful questionnaires to help people check off the things they need to carefully consider.

I found it – for even as I approach 70, I have changed my work but not retired, planning to transition over time – personally valuable as it inspired me to think more carefully about next stages at the same time as it provided me with a practical framework to realise it.

It is all to easy to drift into retirement with no real plans at the same time as we stress over whether we have enough of a nest-egg to meet our needs, themselves often ill-defined. Whilst the latter is obviously important, and the subject of endless commentary, most of us should probably think more about what we want in our retirement and then turn to the resources we might need.

Too many drift in to retirement with a lack of intentionality: we should be asking ourselves what will make our later years purposeful, worthwhile, fun, and relationally rich. Furthermore, the right attitudes, as is the case in all stages of our lives – thankfulness, gratitude, appreciation of our loved ones and the opportunity to theirs in return – will make the world of difference.

Plainly, the author seeks to move his readers from viewing retirement as a passive "reward" to seeing it as an active, purposeful life stage requiring intentional design. He wants us to see that excitement rather than anxiety can be ours if we plan properly, and he encourages readers to stop postponing retirement plans until "later".

Packed with insights, the experience of someone who has worked in the area for many years, and lots of simple old-fashioned wisdom, the book is well written and easy to read.

In summary this is an excellent resource and I commend it to all who are yet to retire, and because it's never too late, to those transitioning to or already in retirement!

The Honourable John Anderson AC FTSE

PREFACE

As a young kid, I wondered what on earth 'old' people did all day. When my parents took me to visit my two grandmothers at their aged care home, I would see old people relaxing in armchairs. They seemed to sit there for eternity. When we left the village, I would notice those same people still firmly ensconced in their chairs... just sitting.

When I was a young adult, I set off on a backpacking holiday across Europe with Clair (whom I married three years later) and two long-time friends, Chris and Rachel. We explored the Greek Islands during the trip, visiting Crete and Corfu. As we strolled through the quaint villages, I noticed 'old' ladies and men sitting on balconies, simply staring into space.

I wondered why these people spent so much time sitting and watching the world go by. It bothered me to some extent... it felt like a waste of time. I couldn't understand how someone could sit idly by. It seemed so aimless and pointless. Even at that young age, I briefly wondered whether that could be me many years down the track, whether I could end up sitting and watching.

Little did I know that decades later, these early observations would shape my understanding of what retirement could and, to be frank, should be.

Later, I started reading various articles about positive ageing, and I realised, to my relief, that life in the mature years could be a joyful, fulfilling time. It is ultimately about freedom of choice. We can choose the path of least resistance and let our lives slip away, or we can actively engage with all that life has to offer and embrace it fully.

Later in life, as I undertook more research into ageing and retirement, I questioned whether waiting around contemplating one's navel was the best way to spend those latter years (currently, often multiple decades).

I also examined specific research papers on people transitioning into retirement. I was surprised and shocked to find that many men keeled over and died within their first six months of retirement. And if they did not succumb to this misfortune early on, there was a high chance they would face a serious illness within five years of retiring.

This was more than just a correlation. Research reveals that the sudden loss of structure, identity, and most importantly, purpose, is literally killing people who should be entering their golden years. I found it most intriguing and illuminating to discover that, to a large degree (putting aside inherited genes), one of the causal factors of premature death was a lack of purpose in the latter years of one's life.

The real motivation for writing this book was the realisation that certain people slip into retirement unintentionally, without a clear purpose. Sadly, many of these people leave this world far too soon, often because they lack purpose as they enter this season of their lives.

It troubled me that many people were floundering and drifting aimlessly through their retirement years, when life could be so much richer, more fulfilling, and more purposeful.

My journey from executive leadership to business and retirement coaching has given me insight into life's key transitions. Whether that's about moving from employee to employer or from career to retirement. I've seen firsthand how these moments can become opportunities for meaningful reinvention.

 AN ABUNDANT LIFE BEYOND RETIREMENT

Coaching prospective retirees who initially asked essential retirement questions, then seeing satisfied clients walk into the sunset with clear plans and a purpose for their future, sparked a thought:

There are only so many people I can positively influence through retirement coaching. If I could capture all the elements of proactive retirement planning, many more people could have their lives positively impacted. When considering the staggering statistics regarding the 'baby boomer' generation progressively retiring, there was a sense of urgency to record my experiences and acquired knowledge.

Considering the 'boomer' generation, by 2030, all 'boomers' (born between 1946 and 1964) will be aged 65 or older! The rapid rise in aging populations is clear. The number of people aged 65 and above is expected to nearly double, from 3.8 million in 2017 to about 6.5 million in 2042. With 10,000 'boomers' retiring daily in many developed countries, we are experiencing an unprecedented retirement tsunami.

The question is, will you be prepared when your time comes? I earnestly believe that after reading this book and intentionally and wholeheartedly applying its principles, you will not only survive retirement but also thrive in what could become the most purposeful and fulfilling stage of your life. That is my wish, hope, and prayer for you.

Unlike the countless books focused on financial retirement planning, this book addresses the other 90% of retirement: your purpose, relationships, health, legacy, and daily fulfilment.

Having enough money to retire is just the entry ticket. Knowing how to live meaningfully is what determines whether retirement becomes your most significant season or your greatest disappointment.

INTRODUCTION

Initially, as a Retirement Coach, I anticipated spending considerable time referring clients to Financial Planners. However, what I discovered was quite different and enlightening. In over 80% of my initial consultations, it was not the finances that needed immediate attention. It was everything else: purpose, identity, relationships, and daily meaning. This revelation was as surprising to my clients as it was to me!

There is a common belief that: *'when I retire, if I have enough money, everything will work out well. I will have all the time I want to do everything I have longed to do.'*

However, when people finally retire, their experience tends to be more complex and varied.

Take Robert, for example.

He had a very healthy superannuation (pension) fund balance, a diverse share portfolio, and a paid-off family home. After working an average of 50 hours per week for approximately 42 years, with compulsory contributions to his superannuation fund at every pay cycle, he felt reasonably secure. He had been given a massive card, signed by all his colleagues in the department. He listened as his managers and coworkers expressed gratitude for his positive impact and loyal, committed service. He felt deeply appreciated and affirmed, making it a moving, emotional experience.

That night, he went home to his wife, who was already dressed and ready to go to their favourite restaurant. Their children and grand-children met them at their local trattoria, where they celebrated Robert's career and ... his transition to what they hoped would be many years of happy retirement.

The next few days were among the most relaxing Robert had ever experienced, knowing he didn't have to go to work on Monday. There were no more work goals, objectives, or meetings to attend. No more reports to be analysed. No more clients to call and no more deadlines. The pressure was off! What a relief!

Though no alarm was set for Monday morning, Robert still woke at his usual time out of habit. Instead of getting out of bed to shower, he turned onto his back, looked at the ceiling, and smiled. When he thought of all those people doing the daily grinding commute, his grin widened into a broad smile. Today marked the start of the rest of his life. It had finally arrived, and he knew it was going to be just great!

By Wednesday, the silence in the house felt deafening. The absence of his phone ringing, emails arriving in his inbox, and colleagues dropping by his office created a void he hadn't anticipated. For the first time in decades, nobody needed him. He also noticed that his wife was becoming somewhat annoyed with his omnipresence at home!

Months later, during our first retirement coaching session, Robert recalled his early weeks in retirement. He said it only took him a few days after retiring to realise that, beyond the financial aspects, he hadn't given nearly enough thought to a retirement plan.

One of the early signs was when he and his wife, Jenny, argued about his retirement goals and how he planned to spend all those extra hours (in Robert's case, an additional 10 hours a day!). Jenny may have been right to provoke him, but Robert found himself becoming defensive. Even before the argument, he'd anxiously wondered how he would spend all this time and make these years purposeful and meaningful... let alone fun.

 AN ABUNDANT LIFE BEYOND RETIREMENT

Another sign was that he'd often catch himself wandering around the house, unsure of where he was headed. He reassured himself that it wasn't a sign of cognitive decline, but it left him pondering how he would keep his mind sharp during retirement. Had it been the wrong decision to retire? The thought was somewhat disconcerting. He had always been a decisive, goal-oriented person, not prone to vacillation, and seldom experienced ambivalence. What was happening?

I continued the conversation with Robert, probing to understand his values and his vision for an ideal retirement. We started outlining what was most important to him, exploring how he wanted to spend his time, his interests and hobbies, his legacy, the type of accommodation he preferred, and the kinds of holidays he wished to have. Before I could emphasise how crucial it was for his thoughts and ideas to align with Jenny's, he passionately interrupted with a question I've heard countless times:

'Why don't they tell you this in all the retirement books?

I responded: *'Everyone thinks it is principally the financial information and tools that they need. And it's the economic aspects that sell books, as this information ties into most people's biggest fear about retirement—not having enough money.*

While the financial component is essential, it is not the only thing we need. In fact, it's not even as significant as most people think. I have worked with people who have far less money in their retirement funds than you have, Robert, but they've gone on to enjoy incredibly fulfilling retirement experiences.'

'Really?' asked Robert, looking surprised and hopeful.

Yes. From my experience, if you have substantial retirement funds, you probably get to go on more holidays each year, stay in luxury hotels, dine at more expensive restaurants, and drive a smarter car. But those aren't what make people joyful, contented, or fulfilled.

Robert's experience is not unique. Research shows that within the first year of retirement, 25-30% of retirees experience what psychologists call 'retirement syndrome'. In this phase, people experience a period of depression, anxiety, and loss of identity that can last months or even years.

Search the internet for books about retirement planning, and you'll find between 25,000 and 35,000 titles, with Barnes & Noble alone listing over 1,200 in their Retirement Planning section. However, 90% of books focus only on financial preparation, leaving a large gap in addressing the psychological, social, and practical aspects of retirement living.

As a Retirement Coach, I can emphasise the importance of financial preparation before and during retirement. However, based on my review of this field, I also recognise that we don't need another book on the economic aspects of retirement planning.

Of the many excellent books on the topic, you have probably already read quite a few. But just in case you've missed any of them, there is a substantial list at the end of this book.

In this book, you will discover what truly contributes to a fulfilling retirement. Throughout each chapter, I will guide you through various aspects and provide a list of thought-provoking questions.

Chapter 1: We will explore your life journey, not for nostalgia, but to identify the patterns, experiences, and achievements that brought you joy and meaning. These insights can serve as a blueprint for planning your retirement years. We will also look at the skills, knowledge, and experience you have gained over the years. Not to pat yourself on the back, but this may guide and inform decisions about your future engagement in your community and society.

Chapter 2: Managing Change addresses the topic of transition and how it functions, particularly as it affects individuals who are thinking of, preparing for, or already in retirement. It will also discuss the stages of change, helping you recognise your current stage and navigate it positively, ultimately leading to a fulfilling retirement.

Chapter 3: We will explore why having a clear purpose isn't just a nice-to-have; rather, it is life-extending. Studies show that retirees with a strong purpose live two to three years longer and report significantly higher life satisfaction.

Chapter 4: Your Well-Being and Resilience will examine what constitutes well-being and resilience. We will look at how well-being contributes to:

- The ability to effectively manage stress
- A clear purpose in life
- Healthy family relationships
- Meaningful connections with others
- A sense of meaning and overall life satisfaction.

When all these factors are in equilibrium, we can say that a person's well-being is positive. We will also examine the body's normal functioning and how to care for it as we age, so we can age gracefully and remain active for as long as possible.

Chapter 5: Your Home. When we approach retirement or are already retired, we face an opportunity and a decision: do we remain in the family home we love, often too big, or consider other options for future accommodation?

Chapter 6: Your Holidays. If we identify the types and nature of different holidays and plan and budget for them, it may lead to a more satisfying retirement.

Chapter 7: Your Work. This chapter examines the value of work, its significance, and the benefits it brings. We explore the potential nature and types of work opportunities available in retirement.

Chapter 8: Your Interests and Hobbies looks at the holistic benefits of hobbies and interests. Engaging in hobbies and interests, along with a sense of purpose in life, can potentially extend our longevity.

Chapter 9: Your Family and Friends. This chapter examines the vital role of friends and family during our retirement years. It also looks at how to cultivate new friendships in retirement.

Chapter 10: Your Legacy. Here, we ask: Do you want to leave a legacy? If so, why and to whom? We then consider the various types of legacies that a person can leave behind.

Chapter 11: Your Final Days. An area that we often avoid discussing, yet a reality we all must face. We will explore how to find acceptance and plan wisely, so we are not a burden on our loved ones.

Chapter 12: Developing Your Retirement Plan. This chapter brings together all our reflections, thoughts, discussions, and knowledge to form a concrete retirement plan.

Chapter 13: Implementing Your Retirement Plan. Implementation or execution is an area that we often find challenging. This chapter supports and guides you in executing your plan effectively and gaining traction.

Chapter 14: Your Retirement Coach examines what retirement coaching involves, its value, and the benefits for you as you intentionally prepare for a flourishing retirement.

Chapter 15: Final Words from Some Wise People will hopefully inspire you about how positive people embrace and make the most of life, living 'other person-centred lives'.

While working as a retirement coach, I have learned how to help people find meaning in retirement. The principles and strategies in this book are practical and straightforward. They have helped people turn retirement from a period of drifting into one of purpose and fulfilment. Through this book, you will explore the key elements and ideas I discuss with my clients (both one-to-one and one-to-two). My sincere hope is that this book will help you create and experience a fulfilling life in your retirement years.

The window for intentional retirement planning is narrower than most of us realise. The habits, relationships, and sense of purpose that will sustain you in retirement ideally need to be cultivated before you retire, but it's never too late, even in retirement!

If, after finishing this book, you believe you would benefit from personalised guidance in creating your ideal retirement plan, please feel free to contact me about retirement coaching.

PART I

THRIVING MINDSET

Part one of this book invites you to reflect on your life's journey so far with gratitude. There might even be a few regrets, and that's okay. None of us, believe it or not, lives a perfect life! Looking back on the past can help inform and guide your thinking and plans for the next chapter of your life.

CHAPTER ONE

YOUR LIFE SO FAR

'Reflection is one of the most underused yet powerful tools for success.'

— Richard Carlson

Yet as retirement approaches (potentially spanning 30-plus years), reflection becomes not just powerful, but essential for designing a life of purpose rather than merely passing time.

As we experience the changing seasons and phases of life, most of us rarely pause to think about what has been, what might be, and what will come. But time keeps moving on, and before we know it, retirement is near. So, if that's where you're at, you have a great chance to deliberately take a moment, maybe at your favourite spot, and reflect on your journey so far. Use this time to think about how you want to prepare for, commence, and enjoy this new chapter of life.

You may be wondering, *'Why would I want to spend time reflecting?' Isn't that just navel-gazing, which will probably lead to introspection if I'm not careful?*

Far from being self-indulgent, reflection is strategic. It's the difference between stumbling into retirement and stepping intentionally into your next stage of life.

Taking the time to reflect on your life as you approach retirement offers several meaningful benefits that can enhance this new stage:

Gaining Perspective

Conducting a self-assessment of the past helps you process your career journey, relationships, and significant life experiences. This can bring a sense of closure to your working years and help you appreciate how far you've come, including challenges you've overcome and the growth you've experienced.

As we reach our 50s and 60s, we can easily forget how we were in our early 20s, when we were starting adult life. It is what I would call the recency effect, where we have a clear perception of our current selves, strengths, weaknesses, giftings, and, hopefully, wisdom. However, we don't necessarily give ourselves any credit for the real growth we've experienced from young adulthood to maturity. For example, how we assessed situations and made decisions in our 20s compared to our 60s. How we learnt from the challenges that life has thrown at us. How we responded to and seized opportunities over the years.

Identifying these moments of growth and maturity may help you appreciate the years and various experiences you have had, recognising how they have equipped you for the future.

Identifying What Truly Matters

Looking back helps clarify your core values and what has given you the most fulfilment. This insight becomes crucial for planning a retirement that aligns with what you genuinely care about, rather than just filling time.

I remember coaching a lady who had worked in the fashion industry for many years. She was kind-hearted, other person-centred, and someone who genuinely valued meaningful, trusting friendships. She mentioned that although she was passionate about fashion and about manifesting her creative talents in the industry, she found the culture superficial and shallow. She always went out of her way to get to know people, taking an interest in their lives. However, this tended to be a one-way street, as most of her colleagues knew very little about her.

As she reflected on what she wanted from retirement, she realised she longed for mutually affirming friends. People who shared her values. She resolved to pursue friendships with people who valued her for who she was and showed a genuine interest in her life. When she came to this realisation, it was like a light bulb suddenly lit up. It was a real 'aha' moment.

Two years later, she had joined a book club, volunteered with a mentoring program, and formed three close friendships with people who shared her values of authenticity and genuine connection. Her retirement became emotionally fulfilling.

Learning From Your Experiences

Reflection allows you to extract wisdom from successes and setbacks. This learning can guide your decisions in retirement and help you avoid repeating unhelpful patterns.

If you look back on your life, you can undoubtedly recall times when you made decisions on a whim or based on your 'gut feel'. These decisions may have resulted in unintended consequences. It may have been a business opportunity that seemed ideal, a person you hired without thorough reference checking, or a car you impulsively purchased without a technical inspection.

Reflecting on the lessons to be learnt from these types of experiences can and should help you make more considered and prudent decisions. Decisions that have the potential to significantly impact your retirement years (for example, where you decide to live).

Specific Skills and Experience Gained

It's important to appreciate that as you approach the final stages of your working life, you will have cultivated and accumulated vast knowledge, skills, experience, and wisdom; often, more than you give yourself credit for.

As you reflect on your working life and career, you will probably agree that it didn't just happen. You will have spent considerable time in preparation: at least 13 years at school and (for an increasing number of people) another three to six years at university.

In addition to formal education, the average person will receive on-the-job coaching and attend internal and external training programs. Most progressive companies have career planning strategies, including career path families and other practices, to support their employees' progression through different roles. Business coaching for potential and existing leaders is increasingly regarded as the most effective way to develop leadership capability (due to its intensive nature and client-driven agenda).

Here is a simple exercise to help you recall the skills, knowledge, and experience you have accumulated over the years. This involves creating your own 'skills inventory'. You are about to have over 2,000 plus extra hours each year to invest. Identifying your skills, knowledge, and experience will help you understand where you could apply these abilities in the future.

Take some time to consider the skills, knowledge, and experience you have cultivated throughout your life:

Within the Workplace

SKILLS	KNOWLEDGE	EXPERIENCE

External to the Workplace (e.g., University, Community Projects, Sports Councils)

SKILLS	KNOWLEDGE	EXPERIENCE

Hopefully, this exercise was helpful and informative as you reflected on your work and community experiences so far. Later in this book, you will have the opportunity to refer back to this chapter to consider how you might utilise the expertise gained in future potential work ventures when you transition.

If you're thinking, *'I'll complete this later,'* remember later becomes never, and never leads to drift. Your retirement planning starts with this exercise, so make sure you schedule a time to complete it!

Processing Unfinished Business

You may identify relationships that require attention, personal goals you want to pursue, or aspects of yourself that you have not fully explored. Retirement offers the time and freedom to address these areas.

A scenario that often arises in coaching is fathers expressing regret about the years lost to not engaging with their children. The song 'Cat's in the Cradle' (Performed by Harry Chapin) is a poignant reminder of this parental lament. An excerpt from the song illuminates this point so clearly:

I've long since retired, and my sons moved away
I called him up just the other day.
I said, "I'd like to see you if you don't mind"
He said, "I'd love to, Dad, if I could find the time"
"You see, my new job's a hassle, and the kids got the flu
But it's sure nice talking to you, Dad.
It's been sure nice talking to you"
And as I hung up the phone, it occurred to me
He'd grown up just like me.
My boy was just like me.

The good news? Unlike the song, your story doesn't have to end this way. Retirement offers a unique window to rebuild and deepen relationships when the pressures of career no longer compete for your attention.

Reflecting on relationships that need restoring helps us make the most of each day, be intentional, and invest in the lives of our adult children, even if they were neglected during those busy working years. Just imagine the deeply rewarding times you can have with adult children throughout your entire retirement journey, which could potentially last thirty-plus years.

Building Confidence For the Transition

Recognising your resilience and adaptability through past changes can boost your confidence about navigating retirement successfully. You have likely traversed major life and/or work transitions before and can draw on those experiences.

This is an ideal opportunity to reflect on times of change in your early career, how you navigated them, and how you adapted to change later in your working life. Undoubtedly, there were things you were good at, but also areas that you found stressful and challenging. The retirement journey is no different; it's a time of significant change. So, if you consider the lessons learnt and the skills gained during those times, they will help you as you transition.

Creating Intentional Direction

Instead of simply slipping into retirement, reflection helps you envision how you want to spend this phase. You can make conscious choices about activities, relationships, and pursuits that will make retirement truly fulfilling rather than just comfortable.

This is a vital point, as it underscores the significance of each of the following chapters in retirement. Acting intentionally and with commitment as you grasp the importance of the themes in these chapters can lead to a thriving retirement.

This reflective process helps you to enter retirement as your most authentic, integrated self, with clear priorities and realistic expectations about what lies ahead.

The skills and experience developed throughout your working life become valuable assets that can significantly enrich retirement in multiple ways:

Problem-Solving and Decision-Making Abilities

Lessons learned in this area have direct application to retirement challenges. Whether it's managing finances, planning travel, dealing with health decisions, or navigating family complexities. Years of analysing situations and making informed choices will serve you well in the future.

Communication and Interpersonal Skills

These skills become especially valuable as you build new social connections, volunteer for causes of interest, or mentor others. The ability to work with diverse people, resolve conflicts, and build relationships opens the door to meaningful retirement activities and friendships.

Project Management Capabilities

The ability to manage projects (big or small) pays dividends when you have to tackle personal goals that may have been deferred during your working years. Whether renovating the family home, organising family history, planning extended travel, or starting a hobby business, the ability to plan, organise, and execute projects becomes personally fulfilling rather than an onerous chore.

Teaching and Mentoring Abilities

The ability to teach or mentor can provide deep satisfaction through formal or informal opportunities to share the expertise you gained during your career. Many retirees find purpose in coaching younger professionals, mentoring students, or leading community workshops, using their knowledge to make a meaningful impact.

Financial and Business Acumen

Whether you have a background in finance or not, having these technical skills proves invaluable for managing retirement savings, making investment decisions, or even starting small entrepreneurial ventures. An understanding of budgets, markets, and business operations helps you make your money work effectively in retirement.

Industry Knowledge and Networks

Networks and networking are crucial for opening doors to consulting opportunities, board positions, or part-time work that keeps you engaged without the full demands of a career. This expertise remains valuable as you enter retirement.

Leadership Experience

Your leadership skills and experience often translate well to community involvement, where organisations greatly benefit from people who understand governance, strategic thinking, and team dynamics.

Technical Skills

Technical skills gained over the years often have personal use. Whether using technology to stay connected with family, managing digital documents, or pursuing online learning, feeling comfortable using different tools can be beneficial throughout retirement.

The key insight is that retirement doesn't mean that your capabilities disappear; it simply means they are being utilised differently. Instead, you gain the freedom to apply them in ways that align with your interests and values rather than external demands. Many people discover that using their professional skills to serve causes they care about provides a more profound sense of purpose than their original career ever did.

As we reflect on what we've learnt, experienced, and lived, we must also look forward to what might be. In times past, people retired, and if they were healthy and fortunate, they enjoyed a limited number of years of relaxation before they passed.

For example, in the 1930s, many workers never actually made it to retirement (in 1935, life expectancy for men was 58 and for women 62). If they did, they would be fortunate to live for another ten years. Today, we have the potential to live much longer.

Centenarians are now Australia's fastest-growing demographic. Concerning people aged 85 and over, the proportion has increased from 0.5% (63,200) in 1970 to 1.1% (190,400) in 1995, and to 2.1% as of 30 June 2020 (528,000). The proportion is expected to rise to between 3.6% and 4.4% in 2066 (ABS 2018, 2020a).

Research also shows that many people live past life expectancy. According to the Australian Bureau of Statistics (ABS), the average retirement age for all retirees (aged 45 and over as of 2022-2023) was 56.9 years. Based on these figures, it's likely that many of these retirees (if in reasonably good health) will enjoy a long retirement.

So, what do all these statistics mean for you? If you retire at 65, you are not planning for five to ten years of leisure; you are creating what could be a 30-year journey. That's longer than many entire careers. The question isn't whether you can afford to retire; it's whether you can afford not to prepare and plan for it.

There is an interesting and surprising story that illustrates the changing nature of longevity across countries. Gratton and Scott, in their book *The 100-Year Life*, tell two such stories about the impact of increasing longevity on structures and systems.

In the past (1950s), it was considered highly unusual for a person to reach 100. It was therefore a noble thing to recognise and reward people who had reached this rare milestone. In the UK, the late Queen and now the King send a letter/card to the centenarian to celebrate the occasion.

In 2006, only one person was responsible for coordinating and distributing the cards. However, as more people lived longer, the team of one expanded exponentially to seven in 2014. With an ageing population in the UK, it has undoubtedly increased further in subsequent years!

Japan, one of the oldest populations (in terms of longevity), faced a different challenge: rising costs! In 1963, they began honouring their centenarians with a gift in the form of a beautiful silver sake dish called a 'sakazuki'.

This worked well in 1963, as only 153 people qualified for this gift. However, by 2014, almost 30,000 such people had received the sake dish. By 2015, the government decided it could no longer afford this burgeoning cost and discontinued the tradition. Without a doubt, many Japanese centenarians would have been unhappy that year.

These stories illustrate a profound shift. Longevity has changed from an exception to an expectation. Your retirement is by no means an epilogue to your working life. It could be an entirely new book!

In concluding this chapter, I would like to share a brilliant quote about living a long, whole life.

From an article in the *National Geographic*: The secrets of the world's longest-lived people:

'If I had a jewel to give to people who want to live long and well, I would tell them to get up early in the morning and go out,' Dr Ferrucci said. *'That is the best gift you can give yourself if you want longevity.'*

You stand at a threshold that previous generations rarely reached. The opportunity to consciously design decades of living after your working life. So, taking the time to reflect will enable the wisdom you have developed over the years to inform your future self.

Reflection requires courage and the willingness to honestly assess what worked and what did not. This is what separates those who thrive in retirement from those who merely survive it.

Reflection Questions for a Thriving Retirement

1. What are you most grateful for in your life so far?

2. What is your biggest regret, or what do you wish you had done differently?

3. What would you have done in your life if you had no fear?

4. What do you wish you'd had the courage to do in your life so far?

5. If you had one piece of advice for someone in their thirties or forties, what would that be?

6. What achievements are you most proud of that have nothing to do with your career?

7. Which relationships have shaped you the most, and how?

8. What were the pivotal moments or decisions that changed the course of your life?

9. What did you believe about yourself at 25 that you've since discovered wasn't true?

10. What life lessons took you the longest time to learn?

11. When in your life did you feel most alive or fulfilled?

12. Consider moments in your work and personal life where you derived the greatest satisfaction and dissatisfaction.

13. We've all received feedback at different junctures; sometimes very affirming and encouraging, sometimes painful, and sometimes discouraging. Consider the feedback you have received that you ultimately found helpful.

14. What are the key things and who are the people that you are thankful for?

CHAPTER TWO

MANAGING CHANGE

'Change is a normal part of our lives, but it's uncomfortable for the vast majority of people because it makes them feel like they've lost control.'

—Mary Jo Asmus

Retirement represents one of the most significant shifts we'll ever experience, from structured days to open calendars, from defined roles to undefined possibilities.

Whether or not you are looking forward to it, the transition from working life to retirement marks a significant change in a person's life. It's comparable to major life events such as getting married, starting your first full-time job, and becoming a parent. There may be days when you feel like you are taking the change in your stride, and other days when it is uncomfortable or even quite scary. For days when the change feels even slightly painful, this chapter addresses change and how it operates, particularly as it affects individuals who are thinking about, preparing for, or already retired.

It will also cover the stages of change, helping you identify your current stage and how to manage it positively, ultimately leading to a fulfilling retirement.

What Do We Think About Change?

In 500 BC, the Greek philosopher Heraclitus said:

'All things change; nothing abides.
Into the same river, one cannot step twice.'

What a prescient statement. Not only is change the only constant, but the rate and frequency of change have increased exponentially since 500 BC.

Whilst facilitating a business workshop, I asked the participants three questions:

1. Who likes change?

2. Who dislikes change?

3. Who would prefer not to change but accept that it is inevitable?

In my straw poll, only 20% reported embracing change, whereas 80% reported resisting or merely tolerating it. Research studies (Change Perception Index and the Luck Readiness Index) indicate that one in three people would avoid change if they could.

The point is that change is not something many of us find easy to embrace, even when given the choice. The good news is that those who learn to navigate change positively are more likely to thrive in retirement, while those who resist it may find the transition challenging.

Change is seldom easy, even in the best of times. However, it is pos-sible if we are intentional and committed to addressing the areas we want or need to change.

Reflecting on the past and assessing what worked well, where we derived satisfaction and when we flourished can provide valuable insights into how we approach the future. There may be regrets or areas we want to change, modify, stop, start, or reduce.

It's never too late to make a change. Consider the Russian writer, Leo Tolstoy, who learnt to ride a bicycle at the ripe old age of 67. Later, we will explore how to approach change during your transition to retirement and offer a practical method for self-coaching through this process.

So Why Do We Resist Change?

We resist change because it is uncertain, and the outcome is unknown. When things remain the same, they feel predictable and safe. Even when small things change, we don't know what will happen next. Sometimes it feels easier to maintain the status quo than to risk a potentially harmful outcome.

In a Harvard Business Review article titled 'Ten Reasons Why People Resist Change,' Rosabeth Moss Kanter offers wise counsel on how business leaders can address these areas of resistance. Many of the reasons she lists apply equally to most of us, regardless of our 'station in life'.

Some of the areas she speaks about:

- Loss of Control
- Excess Uncertainty
- Surprise, Surprise
- Everything Seems Different
- Ripple Effect
- Sometimes, the Threat is Real

Illustrating the impact of a couple of these areas:

Loss of Control: For the first time in decades, you don't have an external structure to organise your days.

Excess Uncertainty: Without a clear career path, the future seems uncertain.

In retirement, each of these resistance factors intensifies. Significantly, you are simultaneously changing your identity, routine, social connections, and life structure.

For many of us, as we have travelled through life, we have maintained relatively healthy control over our lives. We have made choices about the type of career we wanted, where we wanted to live (within a realistic budget), and who we chose to befriend, among other things. However, transitioning into retirement is a whole different ball game.

For some of us, the resistance to that change is all about self-preservation; we avoid facing it by not planning for or thinking about it, thereby avoiding any associated anxiety. The issue with this approach is that, at some point, we will be forced to confront reality, and change will occur, requiring us to respond rather than plan proactively.

What Does This Mean When We Consider the Changes Involved in Retirement?

Each of the areas identified by Rosabeth Moss Kanter (including the final one, 'The Threat Is Real') is significant in considering the changes in retirement.

Retirement represents a complete overhaul of our lives. That's a lot of change, likely to bring feelings of uncertainty and anxiety. Some people don't notice how change affects them until it occurs. Others anticipate the change and attempt to prepare for it.

No matter when you face change-related anxiety, this chapter offers guidance to help you navigate change confidently, embracing it instead of resisting.

The Stages of Change

While pursuing my Master's degree in Coaching Psychology at the University of Sydney, I was fortunate to have the late Dr Tony Grant as one of my lecturers. Exposure to his sharp wit, insightful mind, and dry sense of humour made lectures far more engaging, memorable, and enjoyable. Tony co-authored a book titled *Coach Yourself, It's your life, and what will you do with it?* which offers a very practical framework with specific exercises and a structured approach to creating and maintaining change. A crucial idea is to shift from intention to commitment. Intentionality involves recognising the benefits of initiating change, whereas commitment entails taking action and seeing it through to completion.

When aiming to effect positive change, you need to progress from precontemplation to contemplation, preparation, action, and ultimately maintenance. Certain techniques are effective at specific stages.

Before working through these different stages of change and the helpful tips to consider and adopt at each of the stages, let's look at a straightforward example of how this model works:

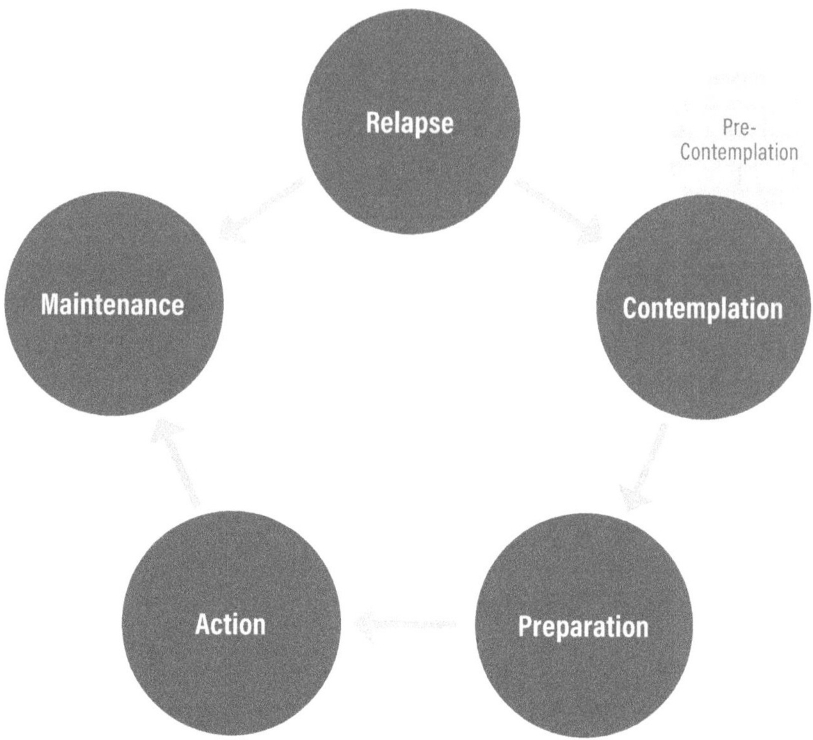

1. Pre-Contemplation

Pre-contemplation is when a person hasn't given any thought to making a change. Therefore, it sits to the side of the model of change.

2. Contemplation

Contemplation occurs when a person starts considering a change they'd like to make. They haven't yet begun acting on it, but they're thinking about it.

3. Preparation

Preparation is when a person begins planning how, where, and when an activity or practice aligned with the desired change will start.

4. Action

Action is when a person starts and consistently repeats an activity or practice connected to the desired change.

5. Maintenance

Maintenance involves creating a consistent routine for the activity and maintaining it over time so that it turns into a healthy habit.

6. Relapse

Relapse is common, so it deserves a place in the 'Stages of Change'. Accepting that relapse often happens means recognising it as ' normal' rather than criticising oneself when momentum with a new change is lost.

In life, obstacles and distractions can get in the way or derail significant initiatives. However, if the person remains committed, they can readily recalibrate and return to 'Maintenance'.

Now that you have a clear sense of how 'The Stages of Change' model works, let's examine it through the prism of someone starting to think about retirement.

Lauren celebrated her 50th birthday with her closest friends at a popular Italian restaurant. As expected, a range of emotions, thoughts, and feelings came to the surface during this milestone. Her friends also made comments about this special occasion! Over a convivial chat with a few glasses of Sauvignon Blanc and a rich Shiraz, her friends shared their thoughts:

'When are you going to slow down and enjoy life more?'

'It's time to smell the roses.'

'You've worked so hard for so long; you deserve to have more time for fun.'

'Time to start thinking what's best next in the life of beautiful Lauren!'

'Have you ever thought about early retirement?!'

As Lauren arrived home and relaxed on the couch, she began to ruminate and reflect on all the conversations. Her mind went to her future... 'What does the next chapter hold for me?' she wondered.

1. Pre-Contemplation

On Saturday morning, several of Lauren's friends called her, and others popped around to belatedly wish her well, some welcoming her to the '50s club!'

As the calls and visitors diminished by the afternoon, she reflected on the night before. She smiled, feeling affirmed by all the supportive comments and some of the frivolity that accompanied such a fun evening.

Though it crossed her mind that she'd be 65 in fifteen years, she wasn't ready to consider retirement in any profound way, so she pushed the reflection aside and moved on with her day.

2. Contemplation

A few years later, Lauren was out to dinner with her friend, Sarah (who was 55). Sarah mentioned that she started 'salary sacrificing' into her super fund ten years prior and had enlisted a financial adviser. A Retirement Coach was also assisting her in working on the many other aspects associated with life in retirement (where to live, hobbies to invest in, travel, her ongoing health and fitness, etc).

Lauren was now 53! Sarah's comments made her think she could do more to plan for her retirement. It was a daunting thought. There was so much to consider. What would she do with her life, especially with all that extra free time, something she had never had since graduating from university?

As Lauren travelled home, her head was spinning with thoughts. It suddenly hit her: it was time to start seriously thinking about what to do about her future. She decided to be proactive and 'take the proverbial bull by the horns'.

That conversation with Sarah was Lauren's tipping point. She realised that the time for thinking about retirement was over. It was time to act!

3. Preparation

Sarah had sent Lauren a WhatsApp message overnight with the name of her Retirement Coach and the name of a website with a plethora of resources on retirement.

She spent most of Sunday morning browsing the website and was impressed by the helpful information and advice. However, it also concerned her a little to think about all the areas she needed to consider and plan for. She reframed her thinking, telling herself she would be proactive and that time was on her side. She felt better after that.

She made a note in her diary that she would call the retirement coach and a financial advisor on Thursday.

4. Action

Lauren attended a session with the Retirement Coach and met with her Financial Advisor. Following the advisor's advice, Lauren commenced salary sacrificing into her super.

Following the initial session, she decided to engage the Retirement Coach for a series of 1.5-hour sessions. After two sessions, she felt inspired and excited about what the future might hold for her… it was not something to be feared but rather a very special stage of life. She had already begun considering where she would live and what type of accommodation she would need in her retirement. She also began researching various volunteering opportunities in Australia and overseas and was excited about several prospects.

5. Maintenance

While she missed the portion of her salary allocated to her super, she kept reminding herself that it would be worthwhile when she moved into her 'third stage of life'.

She was pleased that she had engaged the Retirement Coach, as he kept her on her toes regarding various goals, she had set for herself at previous sessions. Every time they met, he would ask her how she had progressed in her actions (e.g., tasks such as hobbies and interests, future accommodation, volunteer work, health and well-being, her legacy, etc.). Although it was quite demanding, it helped her stay focused and accountable.

She wished she had engaged a Retirement Coach when she was younger!

6. Relapse

While flying back to Melbourne from a business trip to Singapore, Lauren contracted a severe case of DVT. Her doctor advised her to get some solid rest so her body could fully recover before flying again. She was disappointed as she had planned a cruise in Croatia in three months' time.

She did not want to miss this holiday, which she had planned a year earlier with three close friends. So, she dutifully rested, which meant she missed two sessions with her Retirement Coach. She was disappointed but realised her health had to take priority. Her coach wasn't going anywhere; she rescheduled her next meeting for a week after her Croatian holiday.

Tips for Moving Through the Stages of Change

With any desired change, your goal is to reach 'maintenance' and stay there. You may relapse and, as a result, move back a few stages. You might return to contemplation, or perhaps you will go back to preparation as you recommit to the actions needed for your desired retirement.

No matter your stage, recognising which one you are at is empowering because it boosts your awareness of the next steps.

Here are some practical tips to support and motivate you as you navigate change while planning for retirement. Recognise which stage of this model you might be in (e.g. Pre-contemplation or Action) and what could be helpful for you to do to stay focused.

STAGE OF CHANGE	TIPS TO MOVE FORWARD
Pre-contemplation	Spend time being present, considering what you want your life to be. Schedule half an hour weekly to envision your ideal retirement day. What would you do? Who would you spend time with?
Contemplation	Shift your focus to finding the best solution for yourself. Consider the reasons to change rather than not. Examine your options. List what excites you about retirement alongside what concerns you. Often, the excitement outweighs the fears.
Preparation	Don't rush change; instead, develop a plan first. Make a personal commitment to change. Write down your commitment.
Action	Change your perspective. Focus on the future and visualise yourself after you've changed. Focus on how you will benefit and the positive impact these changes will have on you once implemented. Keep reminding yourself of your commitment to change. Keep up the momentum with your milestones and let them inspire you to keep moving forward. Ask a trusted friend to support you by holding you accountable for continued progress toward your desired outcome. Maintain your focus and continue to set realistic actions to avoid relapse. Celebrate your small wins along the way.

Action continued	Set one small retirement-related goal each month. Research volunteer opportunities, try a new hobby, or schedule a health check-up.
Maintenance	Recognise that establishing sustainable change is an ongoing process that demands your discipline and continuous commitment. Build upon the positive impact that your actions have had on your life and continue with small steps of change.
Relapse	Accept that relapse is common and be kind to yourself. Learn from the reasons that caused you to relapse. Reset and get back on track with your actions by reminding yourself of the 'why' behind the change you have initiated.

Unlike other major life transitions, retirement typically lacks specific external deadlines. This means it's up to you to decide how you navigate this change and when to start. However, you don't need to do it alone. In the chapter *Your Retirement Coach,* you will discover that there is help at hand.

Reflection Questions for a Thriving Retirement

1. Do you thrive on change, or do you tend to resist or avoid change if possible?

2. How have you navigated life's changes so far? What did you do that helped reduce stress associated with the change process?

3. What did you discover about yourself during times of significant change?

4. How can you best prepare for the change process involved in adjusting to retirement?

5. Who could you talk to for support during this significant change in your life?

6. What's the difference between the changes you chose versus the changes that were imposed on you? How did you handle each type differently?

7. Looking back, which changes that initially felt difficult or unwelcome ultimately brought unexpected benefits or growth?

8. What early warning signs indicate you're having difficulty with change, and what strategies can help you get back on track?

9. What aspects of retirement change feel most exciting to you, and which feel most daunting?

10. How might losing your professional identity and daily structure affect you, and what can you do to prepare for this?

11. What relationships might change when you retire (colleagues, family dynamics, social circles, etc.), and how will you navigate these shifts?

12. How do you typically respond to uncertainty, and what tools or practices help you stay grounded during ambiguous times?

13. What stories do you tell yourself about ageing and retirement that might be limiting your ability to adapt positively?

14. How can you reframe retirement not as an ending, but as a beginning or transformation?

15. What 'practice runs' or gradual transitions could you try before fully retiring to see how you adapt to change?

16. How will you maintain flexibility and openness to adjusting your retirement plans as circumstances evolve?

17. What resources (books, courses, groups, professionals, etc.) could help you develop your change management skills before retiring?

CHAPTER THREE

DEFINING YOUR PURPOSE

'The purpose of life is not to be happy but to matter, to be productive, to be useful, to have it make some difference that you lived at all.'

—Leo Rosten

'Many people have a wrong idea of what constitutes true happiness. It is not attained through self-gratification but through fidelity to a worthy purpose.'

—Helen Keller

These timeless insights become especially profound when we face retirement, a time when happiness and purpose must be consciously redefined rather than externally provided.

What is Purpose?

For psychologists, purpose is an abiding intention to achieve a long-term goal that is personally meaningful and makes a positive mark on the world. (Greater Good Magazine).

Notice what the above definition excludes: achievement, status, or external validation (areas that are often important during working years). Purpose is deeply personal but outwardly focused. It becomes especially meaningful in retirement, when opportunities to lead a life of significance grow.

As I work with clients, we address the topic of purpose early in the coaching process, recognising its foundational significance to leading a flourishing retirement. I help facilitate them to gain clarity about their purpose. I ask them the following types of questions:

- What is most important to you in your life?
- Who is most important to you in your life?
- How do you want to spend your days, months, and years in retirement?
- What would you like your friends and family to remember you for? What kind of legacy do you want to leave behind?
- You may be blessed with thirty or more years in retirement. What would you like to accomplish in that time, and what experiences would you like to have?

These questions often catch clients off guard because of how personally challenging they are. After decades of external direction, many have never taken the time to deeply consider what they find meaningful. Yet answering them with a good dose of reflection and honesty creates a pathway to a life that is meaningful and rewarding.

Working through these questions and others is foundational to ultimately creating a holistic approach for your retirement. In many cases, these discussions are very challenging and protracted. This is because it is typically a topic that people give little or no thought to in their early years.

Our sense of purpose evolves throughout our lives, often multiple times. For teenagers, it might involve discovering their identity and making friends. For young adults, it could mean building a career and finding a life partner. For mature adults, it may focus on supporting and raising a family, progressing in their career, or accumulating wealth. As you approach retirement, your purpose will likely shift again, and your life's story will continue to change.

In the article 'How Purpose Changes Across Your Lifetime,' Kira Newman explains that purpose is more like an ongoing journey, similar to happiness. It is not necessarily something we aim for; rather, it is something we develop as we go through life. There will be moments when we live in harmony with our purpose and others when we are misaligned. The vital principle is not to lose heart when out of sync, but to recalibrate and refocus.

Why is Having a Purpose Important?

A study by Cornell and Rochester University found that having a sense of purpose and direction in life contributes to happiness and well-being. Having a sense of purpose also adds to overall life satisfaction.

The Centre for Retirement Research (Boston College) found that people with a sense of purpose experience significantly lower stress levels than those reporting little or no purpose. Low stress levels have been directly linked to greater longevity. Therefore, it is highly probable that having a clear purpose may increase one's life expectancy. A retirement filled with meaning and purpose (rather than an extended vacation) and a time of continued personal growth are likely to lead to a more satisfying and meaningful life.

In a study at Harvard's School of Public Health (Association Between Purpose in Life and Objective Measures of Physical Function in Older Adults), Eric Kim found that older adults with a clear sense of purpose were less likely to exhibit reduced grip strength and slower walking speed. He concluded that a sense of purpose was likely crucial for maintaining physical functioning among older adults.

Patrick Hill, Professor of Psychological and Brain Sciences in Washington University's Arts & Sciences Faculty, studied the significance of purpose (Purpose, Aging, Transitions, and Health, or PATH). He discovered that individuals with a strong sense of purpose tend to lead healthier lives, enjoy more fulfilling relationships, and have better sleep patterns.

Eric Kim also found a positive correlation between having a sense of purpose and a reduced risk of heart attack, and therefore, an increase in longevity. (Purpose in life and reduced risk of myocardial infarction among older U.S. adults with coronary heart disease: a two-year follow-up; 2013).

Research from Cornell University shows that people with lower stress levels generally enjoy higher life satisfaction.

In summary, the research examples above are clear and persuasive: Purpose goes beyond making retirement fulfilling; it also may help extend life.

What Happens to Purpose When People Retire?

Many people approaching retirement or already retired feel fear and a sense of loss of purpose. The main source of their sense of purpose was found in their work, so once work stops, what can take its place to give their lives meaning? So, how do we move to a new or renewed purpose in retirement? This is such an important area to grapple with and work through with clear intention, patience, and determination.

People often struggle to envision what their purpose could look like in retirement. A client once said to me, *'I'm worried about retiring as I have no idea what on earth I will fill my day with. At present, my day is full and meaningful in the work that I do, but once I stop, I'm not sure how I'll spend my days.'*

This fear is rational. Without purpose, retirement becomes an extended weekend that quickly loses its appeal. Research indicates that within six months, many new retirees experience feelings of restlessness, boredom, or even depression. The honeymoon phase of sleeping in and having no schedule wears off faster than most expect.

Roman Stoic philosopher Seneca is quoted as saying: *'Once work is removed, most people have no idea how to spend their time.'* This underscores the importance of spending quality time developing a clear purpose in retirement so that this wonderful stage of life is well spent and joyful.

How do You Create Your Sense of Purpose?

Given how easily a sense of purpose can be lost during retirement, it is vital to reflect on and consider your current purpose in life. Is it still relevant to your next life stage, or is there a benefit in adjusting it? Work has broadly defined many people, and their sense of purpose has been strongly tied to it.

Therein may lie the solution. If you reflect on what you were passionate about and what gave you satisfaction and a sense of accomplishment, these may be areas to pursue in retirement. For example, if you derive much satisfaction from supporting customers or clients in your work, you may enjoy volunteering in service organisations or institutions you admire, and which have regular contact with the community.

As you consider your purpose for the next stage of life, there are so many opportunities and positive challenges to consider. Retirement opens new doors, offering the chance to consider various scenarios, including work, leisure, exercise, and giving back to society. These elements contribute to a person's well-being and can help sustain mental acuity and overall physical health.

What will creating a sense of purpose do for you in retirement? Here are some examples of a well-thought-out purpose for retirement:

- My purpose is to be positive and 'other person-centred', engaging in my local community (areas to be decided) through volunteering, pursuing exercise four times a week, and spending quality time with family and friends in my country and overseas.

- My purpose is to give back to society by serving on not-for-profit (NFP) boards, investing in meritorious causes through generous giving, and writing five books.

- My purpose is to mentor young aspiring business leaders and serve in war-torn countries, helping to build the capacity of those communities.

- My purpose is to leverage my 30 years of business experience to mentor emerging leaders while staying physically strong enough to play with my grandchildren and travel to places that have shaped history.

- Having spent my career solving problems for others, my aim is to address community issues through non-profit board service while finally writing the book I've carried in my heart for decades.

Time should be wisely spent understanding your retirement goals and plans. It's important to consider what truly matters to you. It's also vital to rethink the traditional idea of retirement, which is often seen as a time to relax, unwind, and enjoy leisure. There's no need for routines or strict schedules in your day; you can do anything you like. There is certainly value in having leisure time. However, this traditional conception of retirement can become unhealthy over time. It might work in the short term, but in the long run, it can lead to a loss of purpose and, for some people, to idleness and boredom.

For one person, it might be about transitioning from a life of achievement to a life of significance. For others, it might be more about simply living a healthy lifestyle. For another, it may involve reconnecting with family and friends (spending quality time and investing in their grandchildren's lives) and pursuing interests that were not pursued due to time constraints. For some people, pursuing a part-time or casual role may allow them to utilise their vast experience, knowledge, and wisdom. For others, it may involve serving as an active mentor to less-experienced leaders in the industry sector in which they previously worked.

Some individuals who have worked full-time for most of their lives may transition into volunteering, actively giving back to organisations or people in less fortunate circumstances than themselves. This could involve volunteering on NFP boards and/or working in an NFP locally or overseas. This endeavour may include working for short- to medium-term periods each year (e.g., one month or one quarter per annum).

Finally, there will be people interested in all the above.

How tragic it is to hear someone boast that they have only two years, six months, and four days until their official retirement. Life is to be actively embraced and fully lived, not just wished away. Life is for living; there is no dress rehearsal!

Exercise

Now it's your turn to decide. This exercise will help you begin to determine your purpose during retirement.

Helpful Prompts to Get You Started

Establishing or redefining purpose may seem challenging or nebulous. Here are some areas for you to explore to make it a clearer process:

1. Revisit Chapter 1. What valuable skills and experiences have you gained, mastered, and enjoyed utilising? The skills and knowledge you acquire during your career often equip you for later life, including the possibility of giving back. How could your skills and expertise inform your purpose in retirement?

2. Consider the values that you hold dear.

3. Conduct an audit of your strengths.

4. Think about the benefits to society and your well-being by 'giving back' and contributing to your community and/or beyond.

Bringing it All Together
Retirement Purpose Questionnaire & Worksheet

This is the beginning of an ongoing conversation with yourself about what matters most to you. Your answers may evolve, and that is healthy. Purpose is an iterative journey that may take time. This questionnaire will help you discover what truly matters to you, recognise your passions, and develop a plan for a meaningful retirement.

Self-Discovery

1. What have been the most fulfilling aspects of your career and life so far?

2. What activities, hobbies, or interests have brought you joy outside of work?

3. What are some skills or talents you have that you'd love to continue using?

4. What do you value most in life (e.g., family, learning, community, adventure, creativity)?

5. When have you felt most alive and engaged in recent years? What were you doing/experiencing?

A Vision for Your Retirement

6. What does an ideal day in retirement look like for you?

7. Who do you want to spend more time with during your
    retirement?

8. Would you like to explore any new skills or experiences? (e.g.,
    travel, learning a new language, volunteering, starting a new
    hobby, etc)

9. What legacy do you want to leave for your family, community,
    or the world?

Aligning Your Purpose with Action

10. Which of your past experiences can serve as a foundation for
    your new purpose in retirement?

11. What small steps can you take now to start building a
    purposeful retirement?

12. How can you stay motivated and accountable in pursuing your retirement goals?

____

____

Commitment & Reflection

13. Summarise your purpose in a short mission statement:

____

____

____

____

____

14. What is one thing you can do this month to move closer to your retirement purpose?

____

____

____

Viktor Frankl, Holocaust survivor and psychiatrist, wrote these very powerful words: _'Those who have a 'why' to live, can bear with almost any 'how'._ In retirement, you get to choose both the 'why' and the 'how'. This freedom is either retirement's most extraordinary gift or its most significant challenge, so carpe diem!*

*carpe diem means to seize the day or the moment and make the most of it.

Reflection Questions for a Thriving Retirement

1. What is your purpose in life at present?

2. How could your purpose change as you transition to your next stage of life?

3. What do you need to prepare and plan for this purpose to take root? (Who do you need to see, who could advise you and help you, what research may be helpful, what purchases may be relevant, what do you need to apply for?)

4. What activities or moments in your life have made you feel most alive and energised? How might these inform your retirement purpose?

5. What problems in the world or your community do you feel most compelled to help solve?

6. If you had unlimited resources and couldn't fail, what would you dedicate your retirement years to accomplishing?

7. What aspects of your current work or life roles give you the most profound sense of meaning that you would want to continue in retirement?

8. What values are non-negotiable for you, and how will your retirement purpose honour these?

9. What unfinished dreams or interests from earlier in your life are calling for your attention?

10. How do you want to be remembered by your family, friends, and community?

11. What wisdom, skills, or experiences do you have that others could benefit from?

12. How will you balance fulfilment with service to others in your purpose-driven retirement?

13. What role will rest, play, and leisure have alongside your more purposeful activities?

14. How might your purpose need to evolve as your physical abilities, energy levels, or circumstances change over time?

15. What experiments might you try to see if a potential purpose resonates with you?

16. How will you know if you're living your purpose authentically versus just staying busy?

17. What obstacles (internal fears, external circumstances, resource limitations) might prevent you from pursuing your purpose, and how will you address them?

18. Who in your life supports your sense of purpose, and how can they be part of your journey?

PART II
THRIVING RETIREMENT

After examining the past and present and considering your future goals, it's time to concentrate on some important areas of your life. These are the parts you might not have always given enough attention to during your working years.

As you look to the future, consider all the elements of your life as the 'flywheel' of life (or some might say bicycle wheel); that is, we all have spiritual, emotional, physical, intellectual, social, environmental, and financial aspects to our lives. We must continue to grow and maintain each part of our lives as we age.

So, it can be helpful to think of well-being in retirement as a bicycle wheel. Each spoke represents an important part of life. If one of the spokes breaks, it weakens the wheel's strength. Similarly, if you neglect to look after one of these parts of your life, you risk having a negative effect on other areas over time.

CHAPTER FOUR

YOUR WELL-BEING

'Don't simply retire from something; have something to retire to.'

—Harry Emerson Fosdick

'We don't stop playing because we grow old; we grow old because we stop playing.'

—George Bernard Shaw

'Those who think they have no time for bodily exercise will sooner or later have to find time for illness.'

—Edward Stanley

These insights capture a fundamental truth. Well-being in retirement is an active choice to remain engaged with life rather than simply enduring it.

What is Well-Being?

Well-being is the holistic health of an individual, encompassing physical, mental, psychological, and emotional dimensions. It's also about our ability to manage stress effectively, our sense of purpose in life, healthy family relationships, meaningful connections with others, and overall life satisfaction. When all these factors are in equilibrium, we can say that a person's well-being is positive.

Notice that well-being isn't about constant happiness, which is unrealistic, as happiness often proves to be illusory. It concerns resilience, meaning, and the capacity to navigate life's inevitable ups and downs while maintaining overall satisfaction and a sense of purpose.

If we believe you generally lead a flourishing life rather than often feeling depleted, you are likely to report experiencing well-being.

If there is a healthy equilibrium between a person's world and their life, we are more likely to experience well-being, contentment, and, from time to time, a great sense of happiness.

Well-being is a conscious choice: we choose to lead a healthy life, seek out people who will encourage, inspire and intellectually stimulate us, and give back to society and people... or not.

Will You Experience Well-Being in Retirement?

A report by the London-based Institute of Economic Affairs found that retirement increased the chances of experiencing clinical depression by 40% and the probability of having one diagnosed physical ailment by about 60%. The study also found that retirement increased the likelihood of taking medication for these conditions by approximately 60%. That impact was assessed after controlling for age-related conditions (BBC Capital; Bryan Borzykowski, 14 August 2013).

Why do these alarming statistics exist? It is a reality that many people retire *from* something without retiring *to* something. They leave their working life without planning for their retirement. The result? A void where purpose and structure once thrived.

Following this sobering introduction, research indicates high satisfaction among the current Baby Boomer and Builder generations. McCrindle released its latest research article, "The Changing Faith Relationship of Australia" (McCrindle Research Pty Ltd, 2022).

	Gen Z 18 - 27	Gen Y 28 - 42	Gen X 43 - 57	Boomers 58 - 76	Builders 77+
Sense of purpose	44%	39%	40%	55%	66%
Physical health	35%	34%	30%	35%	38%
Mental health	40%	38%	41%	61%	75%
Spiritual wellbeing	45%	43%	42%	55%	66%
Relationships	61%	57%	50%	59%	71%
Work/career	42%	38%	34%	45%	54%
Personal growth	48%	38%	37%	48%	59%
Dealing with stress	29%	28%	33%	52%	65%
Sense of contentment	45%	45%	39%	52%	65%

Source: McCrindle Research Pty Ltd 2022

The infographic reveals higher life satisfaction among Boomers (born 1946-1964) and, in particular, Builders (born before 1946) compared with younger generations, including Gen X (born 1965-1979).

A single factor doesn't determine well-being; it emerges from multiple dimensions of life that work in harmony. The data show how these areas reinforce one another.

The Builders' strong sense of purpose (66% satisfaction) correlates directly with their ability to manage stress (65% satisfaction). When one's sense of purpose is clear, it can positively affect resilience. Similarly, satisfaction in areas like relationships, health, and meaning does not exist in isolation. They collectively underpin overall life satisfaction.

This interconnected pattern holds across generations. Gen Y shows significantly lower satisfaction in both purpose (39%) and stress management (28%), demonstrating how weakness in one area compounds across others.

High life satisfaction in retirement depends on attending to all dimensions of well-being simultaneously. When one area suffers, it causes a ripple effect that undermines others. Most encouragingly, Boomers and Builders demonstrate that cultivating multiple areas, especially a strong sense of purpose (explored in chapter three), fosters a positive upward spiral where strengths in one domain support and amplify satisfaction in others.

This book covers six of McCrindle's nine areas influencing satisfaction, highlighting their significance for well-being and a fulfilling retirement.

It may be helpful to conduct an annual well-being self-assessment, asking yourself how satisfied you are in each area and noting any changes. Recognise that this self-assessment can, if you choose, serve as a personal guide. Your goal is to increase your awareness. Identifying even one area for improvement can, over time and with effort, have a significant impact on your overall well-being.

Well-Being Self-Assessment

The table enables you to perform a brief self-assessment at any time, preferably annually. This can be a helpful assessment to take once you have your Retirement Plan in place (see chapters twelve and thirteen, Developing and Implementing Your Retirement Plan, which cover the purposes of an Immediate, Medium-Term, and Long-Term Retirement Plan).

YEAR _______

CATEGORY	VERY DISSATISFIED	DISSATISFIED	SATISFIED	VERY SATISFIED
Sense of Purpose				
Physical Health				
Mental Health				
Spiritual Well-being				
Relationships				
Work/Career				
Personal growth				
Dealing with stress				
Sense of contentment				

Note: Mark the relevant box for each category

Exercise Guidelines

Once you have completed the table, consider practical actions you could undertake in the areas you rated Very Dissatisfied and/or Dissatisfied. Discussing your thoughts with your partner, family member, or trusted friend may be helpful. A problem shared is a problem halved!

After setting yourself actions to create a positive change in these areas, consider asking someone to support you. They only need to check in every six months or so to see how you are progressing. This helps ensure that your good intentions turn into lasting commitments.

Mental Health Assessment

Another simple way to assess your well-being is to consider where you currently stand on the 'How Am I?' Index (adapted from the checklist; 2018 Mental Health Week, Canadian Mental Health Association [CMHA]).

Naturally, we all desire to lead a flourishing life. However, sometimes events happen beyond our control (e.g., redundancy, loss of a family member, empty-nest syndrome, the passing of a much-loved pet, a change in one's health, a fractious relationship, etc.). Or we may have reached a plateau in our lives, where enjoyment is no longer present, or we're stuck in a 'liminal space' or 'rut' and cannot transition effectively.

Mental health is a spectrum and a continuum; knowing where you stand today helps you make informed choices to move toward a state of thriving. Most importantly, seeking help when you know you need it is a courageous and wise decision.

This simple index provides a quick way to assess the state of your mind and heart.

How am I?

	THRIVING	SURVIVING	DISTRESSED	UNWELL
1. Mood	Normal fluctuations in mood/ frequent positive emotions	Some nervousness, irritability, sadness	Frequent anxiety, anger, sadness, irritability, pessimistic	Persistent & excessive anxiety, easily enraged, depressed mood
2. Sleep	Quality rest and sleep patterns	Trouble falling a sleep/waking up at wee hours	Restless or disturbed sleep	Unable to fall or stay asleep
3. Energy	Physically well, full of energy	Tired/low energy Muscle tension, headaches	Feeling numb, hopelessness Frequent aches & pains	Exhaustion, physical illness
4. Social	Engaged at home & work Socially active with high quality connections	Decreased engagement at work & home Decreased social activity	Social avoidance or withdrawal	Isolation, avoiding social events
5. Work	Sense of achievement Consistent performance Sense of purpose	Procrastination Forgetfulness	Decreased performance Increased alcohol/ substance use	Unable to perform duties, absenteeism Frequent alcohol/subs

SOURCE: Adapted from the Canadian Mental Health Association

If you're in the first zone, you are most likely flourishing, and as the category says, 'Thriving'. However, if you feel yourself sliding down the scale from 'Surviving' to 'Distressed' and, ultimately, to where you feel 'Unwell', then that's a red flag for you.

If you frequently tick the 'Distressed' or 'Unwell' categories, you are advised to see your GP. During your appointment, the doctor may discern that it's most appropriate to refer you to a mental health professional (counsellor, psychologist or psychiatrist). In such situations, the intention is to seek professional support to restore positive well-being, or, as noted earlier, 'thriving'.

Sometimes, when life becomes overwhelming and stressful, we can slip into thinking the following thoughts:

- 'These thoughts and feelings will never pass.'

- 'I can't do this.'

- 'I can't afford the time to attend sessions; life is too busy.'

- 'What will my family think if I start seeing a therapist?'

These unhelpful thoughts are far too common among many of us when we encounter such thoughts and emotions. The critical refrain when our self-talk constantly leans into these negative thoughts and feelings should be: *I will benefit from seeking support by talking to someone.'*

Prevention is Better Than Cure

A healthy principle regarding our well-being is that 'prevention is better than cure'. As humans, we have a propensity to be stoic and say to ourselves, *'We'll get over this; it may just take a little time, so I'll leave it for now.'* So, if you believe that you are moving from 'Surviving' to 'Distressed', that's the time to see someone so that you don't remain in the 'Distressed' category or regress to the 'Unwell' category. The key is to be proactive rather than reactive.

If we have a toothache, we'll make an appointment with the dentist; if we experience persistent headaches, we'll see our GP. The point is that our mental well-being is just as important as our physical well-being. We are interconnected beings, and one aspect of ourselves tends to affect other aspects. A person's mental well-being deserves the same attention as their physical health, perhaps more so, since it affects everything else.

We will inevitably feel melancholic from time to time throughout life; that's the normal rhythm of life. When that feeling persists, proactive measures are needed to prevent further decline.

What is Optimal Health?

Michael P. O'Donnell (2009) states that our 'optimal health is a dynamic balance of physical, emotional, social, spiritual and intellectual health.' To attain and maintain optimal health (relative to our circum-stances), we face the challenge of ushering in changes in how we lead our lives. We need to educate and motivate ourselves to create sustainable patterns of behaviour that will ensure we make healthy choices in all aspects of our lives.

This dynamic balance concept is crucial. Aiming for perfection in every area is unattainable. However, the goal is to achieve equilibrium, in which strengths in some areas can temporarily compensate for challenges in others.

This image illustrates the interconnection between the various categories related to optimal health:

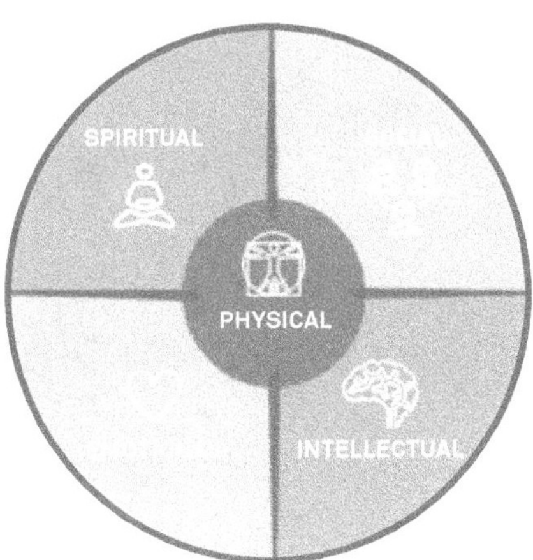

Michael P. O'Donnell (2009). Definition of Health Promotion 2.0: Embracing Passion, Enhancing Motivation, Recognising Dynamic Balance, and Creating Opportunities. American Journal of Health Promotion: September/October 2009, Vol. 24, No. 1, pp. iv-iv.

The Well-Being Audit

As you start to contemplate the future and reflect on the interconnectivity reflected in the above diagram, try completing the well-being audit that follows:

- Looking at the different areas in the table below, which ones currently provide you with high meaning and satisfaction? Which areas are low at present, but ones that you would like to be high in the future, as you appreciate their importance in your life?

- For each area, rate your current **level of importance** to you on a scale of 1–10 (1 = little or no importance and 10 = vitally important).

- For each area, rate your current **level of satisfaction** on a scale of 1-10 (1 = very dissatisfied and 10 = fully satisfied).

For example, you indicated that Friends and Family are very important to you (#10). On the satisfaction scale, you rated yourself 2, indicating a high level of dissatisfaction. This suggests that Family and Friends are very important to you, but they currently bring you very little satisfaction.

Therefore, what goals and actions do you want to commit to increase your level of satisfaction and meaning in this area?

Your Personal Well-Being Audit

AREA	DESCRIPTION	IMPORTANCE 1-10	SATISFACTION 1-10
SOCIAL			
Family and Friends	Could be looked at together or separately.		
EMOTIONAL			
Significant Other	Could be 'Life Partner', close 'Relationship'.		
INTELLECTUAL			
Career	Owning a Business, part-time Work, or Volunteering.		
Personal Growth	Could include Learning, Self-Development.		
PHYSICAL			
Health	Emotional, Physical Fitness, Spiritual, Well-Being. This area could be split into multiple categories.		
Fun & Leisure	E.g. Sports, Hobbies, Interests, Passions, Travel, etc.		
SPIRITUAL			
Spiritual	Initiating, following or becoming further engaged in a particular Belief/Faith.		
OTHER			
Home Environment	Could include the Home, Unit, Land (Sea/change!).		
Finances	Could be Financial Well-Being, Financial Security.		

Wellness Versus Well-being

You may think this is about semantics; however, there is a clear distinction between wellness and well-being. Wellness is about avoiding illness; well-being is about thriving. In retirement, you want both, but well-being is the higher goal because it encompasses meaning, connection, and purpose alongside physical health.

What About Resilience?

The American Psychological Association (APA) defines resilience as the process and outcome of successfully adapting to complex or challenging life experiences, especially through mental, emotional, and behavioural flexibility and adjustment to external and internal demands.

How we adapt to these different circumstances depends on multiple factors. For instance, our outlook on life in general (positive, negative, neutral, etc.), access to close friends and family members (nuclear and/or extended) who may be a source of support. Additionally, our awareness of and ability to utilise strategies for addressing life's challenges will be beneficial.

As we approach retirement, we will encounter significant changes that can be a major source of stress. Work provides many social and psychological benefits.

When we retire, the areas of work that once provided a strong sense of meaning, belonging, and purpose will no longer be present. During our working life, we have a clearly defined purpose and structure for each day. We also benefit from social interaction and encouragement from others (in most cases!). In retirement, the story is different. We suddenly have all this time on our hands, which can become a source of stress.

So, how can we develop the resilience muscle?

Most of us have gone through traumatic events, losses, hardships, and other challenges in our lives. Though these experiences are often unpleasant, they can teach us coping skills. Think about how you managed those storms and what practices and techniques you used to help you. How did you adjust to these challenges and opportunities, and who supported you? Building and maintaining healthy relationships is an invaluable way to develop resilience. Friends who have experienced similar hardships or challenges can be a significant source of support during difficult times. They can be empathetic and help us broaden our perspective on whatever situation we are experiencing.

When we experience a real hardship, such as losing a loved one, it's only natural that there may be a tendency to retreat, and that's ok. However, it is equally important to 'press in' to close friends and family who will provide practical and emotional support. Sharing our emotional states with trusted friends and family can help provide a helpful perspective.

If things become tough, seeking professional help from a counsellor or therapist is advisable rather than soldiering on alone. An experienced professional can provide support and assist you in identifying appropriate coping mechanisms.

As mentioned earlier, the key to a rewarding retirement is to identify your purpose and pursue it. What are the things, people, hobbies, experiences, etc., that will help bring you joy and fulfilment in retirement? Achieving a clear understanding of your life's purpose will enhance your resilience. Purpose is essential for a satisfying life; therefore, be intentional and dedicated to taking time to reflect on it. When you experience difficult times or feel demotivated, remind yourself of your purpose and refocus by setting simple, practical goals that are important to you.

Health and Well-being in Retirement

Looking after yourself through regular physical activity, following a nutritious diet, adopting a positive mindset, reducing stress and ensuring consistent sleep patterns are fundamental pillars of health. Never underestimate the importance of these areas, as they promote longevity and allow you to flourish in retirement.

As we age, our bodies undergo natural changes, and we may face various health challenges later in life. Therefore, we must take care of our bodies and overall health. Some of us are fortunate to have inherited genes that help us lead relatively healthy lives. If that's you, taking care of your body remains vital. If your inherited genes are not your friend, ensure you adopt a robust and sustainable healthy regime by following the advice below, as well as that of your doctor, dietitian and exercise physiologist.

Mindset

Adopting a positive mindset and outlook on life is beneficial and helps us persevere during challenging times. Similarly, reflecting on the small and large things for which you are thankful helps sustain a positive mindset.

Recognising that humans generally dislike change and that, as we age, it becomes more difficult rather than easier, we need to accept this significant life transition rather than resist it. Accepting this change, or even better, embracing it, will undoubtedly strengthen our resilience in various ways.

In his book *The Seven Habits of Highly Effective People*, Stephen Covey discusses the circles of control, influence and concern. I think it's helpful to add a fourth circle: 'no control'.

We control when we go to bed at night and get up in the morning, what we wear, and whether we brush our teeth.

We can exert influence by writing to our local council or to a member of parliament about issues that are profoundly important to us.

We can naturally be very concerned about the state of the economy, world peace, wars, climate change and many other things. However, we cannot effect change in these areas.

We have no control over ageing and little or no control over whether we eventually stop working, although some people do work until the day they die. So, instead of fighting this change, we'll be much better off accepting it as a positive reality.

A Healthy Diet

Nutrition becomes increasingly important as we age, supporting vitality and promoting longevity.

Fibre is essential for optimal health. Aim for 25-30 grams daily from whole grains (brown rice, quinoa, wholemeal bread), legumes, nuts, fruits and vegetables. Fibre supports regular bowel movements, helps control blood sugar levels and can lower cholesterol. It also plays a crucial role in maintaining a healthy gut.

Think of your gut as home to trillions of bacteria. Beneficial bacteria support digestion, immune function, and overall health. To increase beneficial bacteria, include probiotic-rich foods daily. Yoghurt is an excellent choice, as are fermented foods like sauerkraut, kombucha, kimchi and miso.

These good bacteria need food to survive and multiply. That's where prebiotic fibres come in. Foods like onions, garlic, leeks, asparagus, bananas and oats feed your beneficial gut bacteria and keep them thriving.

Your gut and brain communicate with each other through nerve signals. When you nourish your gut with fibre, prebiotics and pro-biotics, research shows it can lift your mood and support mental clarity. A healthy gut supports a healthy mind.

Protein needs increase as we age because our bodies become less efficient at building and maintaining muscle. Aim for approximately 1-1.2 grams of protein per kilogram of body weight daily. As a simple guide, protein should fill roughly a quarter of your plate at each meal. Quality sources include fish, lean meats, eggs, dairy, nuts and legumes.

When you combine adequate protein with resistance exercises like lifting weights or using resistance bands, you'll maintain muscle strength and independence. Strong muscles also reduce your risk of falls and protect your bones.

Dairy products are particularly valuable because they provide both protein and calcium. This is especially important for women post-menopause, when bone density naturally declines due to lower oestrogen levels.

Healthy fats from extra-virgin olive oil, avocados, eggs, nuts, seeds, and fatty fish like salmon protect your heart by helping lower cholesterol and reduce inflammation throughout your body. These same fats are vital for brain health, too.

Regular consumption of oily fish is linked to slower cognitive decline, better memory, and a reduced risk of dementia, so aim for 2-3 servings per week. The fats in olive oil, avocados and nuts also support healthy blood flow to the brain and help reduce inflammation that can affect cognitive function.

Fruits and vegetables should fill half your plate at each meal. Aim for at least five serves daily. They contain natural compounds called antioxidants that protect your cells from damage and may help prevent chronic diseases. Focus on variety and colour. Berries, leafy greens, tomatoes and bright vegetables provide the widest range of protective benefits.

The Mediterranean diet brings all these elements together naturally and has strong scientific evidence for supporting healthy ageing. Numerous large studies show that people who follow this eating pattern have lower rates of heart disease, better brain function and live longer, healthier lives.

Physical Activity

Staying physically active is essential for maintaining strength, independence and vitality as we age. Regular exercise protects against chronic disease, supports mental health, maintains mobility and helps preserve cognitive function.

Australian guidelines recommend adults aim for:

- 2.5 to 5 hours per week of moderate intensity activity such as brisk walking, golf, cycling, mowing the lawn or swimming (about 20-40 minutes daily), or
- 1.25 to 2.5 hours per week of vigorous activity such as jogging, resistance training, aquarobics, fast cycling or team sports (about 10-20 minutes daily), or
- A combination of moderate and vigorous activity
- Muscle-strengthening activities such as squats, resistance bands, lifting weights or heavy gardening on at least 2 days per week

Muscle-strengthening exercises are particularly important as we age. They maintain bone density, prevent falls, support joint health and preserve your ability to perform everyday tasks like carrying groceries or getting up from a chair.

Beyond the physical benefits, exercise triggers neurochemicals that enhance well-being. Physical activity releases endorphins, which create feelings of pleasure and act as natural pain relievers. It boosts dopamine, the 'feel-good' chemical that drives motivation and focus, giving you a sense of accomplishment. Regular exercise helps maintain healthy serotonin levels, which regulate mood and sleep patterns. Combined with sunlight exposure and nutritious foods creates optimal conditions for mental and emotional health.

Choose activities you enjoy, whether that's swimming, dancing, gardening or walking with friends. If you currently do individual activities, consider joining group classes or team sports such as tennis, golf or lawn bowls. Many clubs organise social events alongside physical activity, providing valuable connection and the oxytocin boost from positive social interaction. Start small and build gradually. Even small increases in activity make a meaningful difference.

Consistent Sleep

Sleep is often overlooked, yet it plays a vital role in healthy ageing. Most adults need seven to eight hours of quality sleep each night for the body to restore and repair the brain, cells and muscles effectively.

Poor sleep patterns can develop easily. Late nights socialising, working long hours, scrolling through devices or binge-watching favourite shows can all disrupt our natural sleep cycles. Over time, inconsistent sleep takes a toll on memory, mood, immune function and overall health.

The foundation of good sleep is consistency. Going to bed and waking up at the same time each day, even on weekends, helps regulate your body's internal clock. This doesn't mean giving up your social life or hobbies. It means being intentional about protecting your sleep and recognising it as essential to your well-being.

Quality sleep supports sharper mental acuity, better emotional resilience, stronger immunity and faster physical recovery. It also plays a crucial role in memory consolidation, helping you retain new information and skills. For older adults, adequate sleep is linked to reduced risk of cognitive decline, better balance and coordination, and improved overall health outcomes.

Reducing Stress

Managing stress well supports healthy ageing in numerous ways. When we understand how stress works in our bodies, we can take practical steps to protect our health and maintain vitality.

When we experience stress, our adrenal glands produce cortisol, the body's primary stress hormone. In short bursts, cortisol is beneficial. It mobilises energy, sharpens memory and helps us respond effectively to challenges. The key is learning to activate this response when needed and then return to a calm, balanced state.

Stress also triggers the release of adrenaline and noradrenaline, which increase heart rate, blood flow, and alertness. This gives us the energy and focus to handle demanding situations.

The good news is that we have considerable control over our stress response. While short-term stress can enhance performance, chronic stress can lead to inflammation, sleep difficulties, high blood pressure and reduced immune function.

There are many effective strategies to manage stress. Regular physical activity, meditation, and spending time in nature, away from electronic devices, can be restorative. Practising gratitude during meditation may help mitigate cortisol's effects. Social connection is also beneficial. Physical touch, like hugging, triggers oxytocin, a hormone that reduces anxiety and promotes feelings of warmth and calm. Activities involving social interaction create positive feelings and strengthen relationships.

By actively managing stress, you create the conditions for better sleep, stronger immunity, sharper thinking and greater resilience.

Protecting Your Brain Health

In Australia, dementia is the leading cause of death in women and the second highest for men (coronary heart disease is the number one cause). In the United Kingdom, dementia is the number one cause of death.

Leading causes of death in Australia in 2023, by sex: number and crude rate

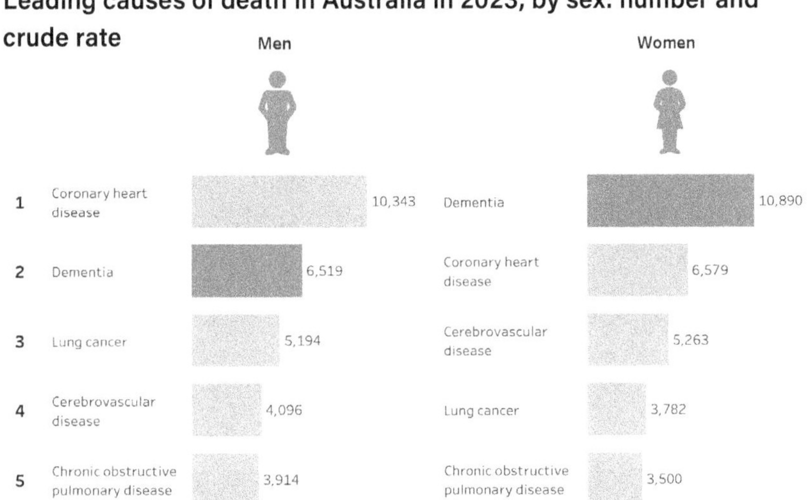

Source: AIHW analysis of the National Mortality Database.
https://www.aihw.gov.au

The good news is that the lifestyle factors we've discussed, nutrition, physical activity, quality sleep and stress management, all work together to protect our brain health as we age. These aren't separate pillars of health. They're interconnected elements that support cognitive function and may reduce the risk of dementia.

There is encouraging news in the *Dementia prevention, intervention, and care: 2024 report of the Lancet standing Commission.* As people are living longer, more people are living with dementia. However, there is hope in that if one is able to eliminate the 14 risk factors (as outlined in the infographic), up to half of all dementias can be theoretically eliminated.

The report is worth reading, as it provides practical mitigating actions one can take regarding the 14 risk factors.

We have already discussed the importance of regular exercise and its numerous benefits, particularly for cardiovascular health. Let's now consider how we care for our brains into old age.

The National Institute of Aging (NIH), a U.S. Department of Health and Human Services division, produced an article entitled 'Cognitive Health and Older Adults'. In it, they describe steps to maintain our cognitive health:

- Take good care of your physical health.
- If you have high blood pressure, manage it effectively.
- Maintain a healthy diet.
- Stay physically and mentally active and on the move.
- Maintain strong involvement in social activities, including friends and family.
- Monitor your stress levels.

The article is thorough and well worth reading.

Regular activities help us maintain physical, emotional and cognitive health. This advice is straightforward. The challenge is to be intentional and disciplined in participating in these many and varied beneficial activities.

Population attributable fraction of potentially modifiable risk factors for dementia

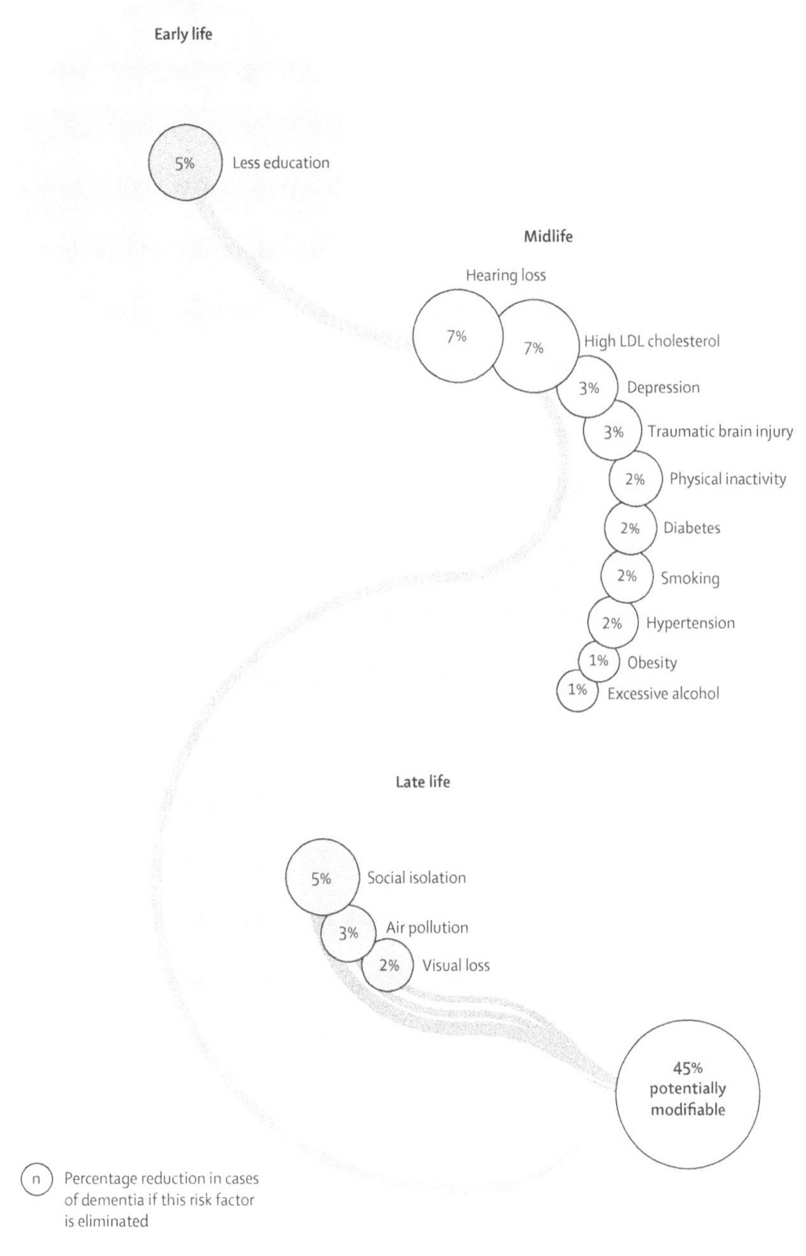

Taking Action

Now is a good time to schedule a comprehensive medical check if you haven't had one recently. Annual health checks provide peace of mind and help detect potential issues early. Blood tests and other examinations can detect many cancers and health problems. Set a recurring reminder in your diary to book your checkup so you won't forget and miss a year.

Well-being in retirement is a journey you choose daily. Every decision about how you spend your time, who you spend it with and what you focus on either contributes to or detracts from your overall well-being. The power to thrive is a conscious choice that only you can make.

Reflection Questions for a Thriving Retirement

1. Now that you've reflected and completed the well-being audit, prioritise the top three areas where you most want to create change.

    i.

    ii.

    iii.

2. What is it that you want to change in each of these three areas? What are you willing to do to bring about positive change in these areas?

3. In what ways did you exercise resilience during your working life; what behaviours did you manifest in those situations?

4. Considering your transition to retirement and the challenges you will inevitably encounter; how will these behaviours help you to be resilient and maintain well-being?

5. When was your last medical check-up?

6. When do you intend to book your next medical check-up?

7. How healthy is your diet right now? Do you need to make changes to it? If so, when will you start?

8. How much coffee and/or tea do you consume now? Consider setting a challenge to cut back by at least x cups per week.

9. On average, how many hours of sleep a night do you have at present?

10. What form/s of exercise do you participate in, and at what frequency?

11. What activities or practices help you manage stress and maintain emotional balance?

12. How do you currently handle feelings of loneliness, boredom, or loss of identity, and what strategies might you need in retirement?

13. What role does spirituality, meditation, or mindfulness play in your well-being, and how might you cultivate this in retirement?

14. How do you maintain optimism and positive thinking during challenging times?

15. Who are the people in your life who energise and support you? How will you maintain and strengthen these relationships in retirement?

16. What new social connections or communities do you want to build in retirement?

17. How comfortable are you with asking for and receiving help when you need it?

18. What activities keep your mind sharp and engaged? How will you continue challenging yourself intellectually in retirement?

19. What new skills or knowledge areas would you like to explore that could contribute to your cognitive health?

20. How do you balance stimulating activities with restorative downtime?

21. What health screenings or preventive measures are appropriate for your age and family history?

22. How are you preparing for potential future health challenges or mobility changes?

23. What role do you want your family or friends to play in supporting your health and well-being decisions?

24. How does your current living environment support your well-being goals? Do you need to make any adjustments?

25. How much time do you spend in nature, and how might you increase this in retirement?

26. What boundaries do you need to set to protect your well-being from negative influences or energy-draining situations?

27. How will you track your progress on your well-being goals and adjust your approach as needed?

28. Who could serve as an accountability partner in your retirement journey?

CHAPTER FIVE

YOUR HOME

'Home is where the heart is.'

—Joseph C Neal

But retirement raises a fundamental question: Is the home that served your family life the right home for your retirement? The answer isn't always obvious.

Home is where happy memories are created. Home is a warm, safe, and loving place. It is where we have our families to love us, take care of us, and guide us through our journeys.

A home is also a sanctuary where we feel safe and secure. A place we are very familiar with and where we know each nook and cranny, every smell, and every sound. Where the light comes in in the morning, and where it exits in the afternoon.

The well-known saying, 'home is where the heart is,' can be especially true for people who have lived in one home for many years and raised a family there.

In later life, the typical situation is that the children have grown up, spread their wings, and left the nest. You might find yourself wandering around in that empty home and pondering whether it still fits you. What was once the ideal house now feels like a big place to maintain for just one or two people.

This is all about purpose. The home that once buzzed with family activity can feel hollow when its primary function disappears. Suddenly, you find yourself maintaining four bedrooms for the memories rather than living life to the fullest.

But it's hard to let go. Many of my clients, when discussing their homes, share with me the many special memories, experiences, laughter, tears, and celebrations they have had. They have so much to hold onto, but at the same time, all those bedrooms are filled with all that STUFF. Sound familiar?

Do we remain in the family home we love, which is often too large, or do we look at alternative options for the future, potentially more suitable accommodation?

It's an important decision that shouldn't be made based on emotions. Instead, it should be carefully thought through rationally and logically.

This decision will likely be one of your biggest financial transactions in retirement, greatly affecting your daily quality of life for many years. It warrants the same careful analysis as any major business or life choice, and perhaps even more, because it cannot be easily reversed.

So, it's not something we should rush into, as it will likely have significant consequences across many levels and areas, including but not limited to:

- Potential funds from the sale of the home that can be transferred to superannuation.

- Making sure you still have room for visitors or perhaps grandchildren.

- Decide whether to sell, renovate, or sell as is.

- Ability to purchase the next home with the same amount of money (or less) secured from the property.

- If purchasing in a townhouse or block of units, will the pension be able to cover rising body corporate levies in the medium term, etc?

- If changing accommodation, whether to remain in the same area or to consider changing suburbs, states, or even possibly countries.

The Timing Question

When should you move? The million-dollar question.

Some experts suggest making housing decisions early in retirement while you are still healthy and adaptable. Others recommend waiting until you have a better understanding of your retirement lifestyle needs.

For some, when the last of the kids leaves the family home, it becomes a prompt to think about future property decisions.

There's wisdom in every approach, so the key is to be intentional and thoughtful rather than impulsive and reactive.

Where Could You Live?

Before we discuss where you should live based on your personal needs and preferences, let's explore what's possible. In working with clients who are designing their ideal retirement, I have heard a wide range of ideas.

Here are just some of the ideas and options I've heard from clients:

- *'Over the past 25-plus years, we've enjoyed many special long weekends and summer holiday breaks at seaside holiday rentals, and oh, how tempting it might be to sell up and buy a little cottage by the sea!'*

- *'There have been some memorable holidays in the hinterland, mountains, and the great outback; simple country living remains just as appealing. Imagine the savings after selling the family home in the city and relocating to a more affordable rural property, even though certain regional areas experienced relatively high growth during the COVID years.'*

- *'A significant downsize to a townhouse, unit, or small cottage may prove to be a more effortless and less painful transition for us than the big move to the coast or the mountains.'*

- *'We tend to be more cautious and believe that a long-term accommodation plan is wise. We expect to sell the home and purchase an independent living unit in a retirement complex. This will enable a transition to low-care and, eventually, high-care support accommodation as needed.'*

- *'I am considering moving to one of my favourite European countries. The South of France and Tuscany hold many happy memories. I may have to enrol in a language school, but I will have plenty of time to do so!'*

- *'We have investigated the prospect of a reverse mortgage to unlock the equity in our home, recognising that residential property is likely to appreciate in 25-30 years. Upon sale, there will likely be a credit balance for our beneficiaries. We are realistic about this idea and understand that we need to do our due diligence before proceeding.'*

- *'We have decided to initially rent our principal property and possibly rent another property for less than our rental income (which could even turn out to be our retirement home). This will naturally provide us with passive disposable income.'*

- *'Our preferred investment strategy is a diversified share portfolio. We do not consider property the optimal investment option. Consequently, we spent most of our adult lives renting. We plan to keep renting as we always have, although we might change homes.*

Where Should You Live?

There's no right or wrong answer as to what to do about your accommodation and where you might live in your third stage of life.

As shown in the list above, options are nearly limitless. No matter where clients want to live, I help them evaluate whether they should stay put or consider a different type of dwelling.

There is a plethora of stories about people who have fallen in love with the idea of living in a seaside home. They sell their home in their metropolitan city and purchase a home or unit on the coast. The first few months are remarkable, with swimming, trying all those new restaurants, and incredible coastal walks. Then reality sets in, they're sitting in their lounge watching the roaring surf, and the wife turns to her husband and says:

'This is a magnificent place, but we don't know anyone here, and our children (and grandchildren) are back in our home city. I miss my family and wish I could visit them by car, but it's just too far! Should we go back?'

However, the property market back home has appreciated further since they sold, so returning may be financially prohibitive, not to mention the additional fees associated with selling and purchasing. They may be stuck now, possibly trapped in a situation they did not fully consider before moving.

This scenario occurs thousands of times each year. The dream turns into a prison because they fell in love with a holiday destination without thinking of it as a permanent home. Holidays are planned experiences, but everyday life involves grocery shopping, doctor visits, and Tuesday afternoons when the surf isn't great.

To help you make a wise choice about where to live during your retirement years, here are several factors to consider:

- Would you be better off staying in the family home, at least for the foreseeable future? You're a keen gardener and will cherish the opportunity to keep those fingers green.

- How important is it to be close to your children and friends? If grandchildren are running around now (or hopefully, they will be very soon), this may strongly influence your decision about where to live. However, remember that grandchildren also grow up and pursue their own lives as young teenagers.

- Do you want to continue working part-time, casually, and/or as a volunteer, possibly in a different job? Will remaining in a metropolitan area be necessary to secure your desired work opportunities?

- You may want to join a few boards and actively participate in the community. You may also be interested in travelling overseas at least once a year. Proximity to a city with an international airport may be vital to you.

- Will selling your home free up surplus capital that can supplement your superannuation?

- Living in a complex or a retirement village will mean not having to worry about maintaining your property; is this important to you?

- How appealing is it to know you can stay in an independent living centre where you can close the front door and lock it, travelling with complete peace of mind?

- Proximity to healthcare (how important is it to be near your current doctors?).

- Maintenance requirements (are you ready to give up gardening, or do you still crave it?).

- Transport and mobility (will you always drive? Is public transport available?).

- Existing support networks (friends who will visit versus friends you may lose touch with).

- Family access (can children visit easily? Will grandchildren want to stay over?).

- Community engagement opportunities (volunteering, clubs, activities).

- Capital release potential (how much equity can fund your retirement?).

- Ongoing costs (body corporate, maintenance, council rates).

- Future flexibility (can you easily move again if circumstances change?).

Before falling in love with any of the above options, it may be prudent for you to try this structured approach and then review your options and preferences:

- Stay in your preferred area or accommodation temporarily, renting for 3-6 months.

- Visit the area during quieter times, like winter, weekdays, or school terms.
- Plan a typical week—where will you shop, exercise, socialise?
- Calculate your true living expenses (not just the purchase price, but all ongoing costs).
- Test the commute to family and essential services (how close is public transport to where you might live?).

There are likely other factors that may not have been listed here. It is recommended that you take time with your partner or a trusted friend to brainstorm additional factors to think about when deciding where to live.

This decision is too important and complex to make alone. Think about forming a small advisory team that includes a Retirement Coach to help you explore your options, choices, and decisions; a financial adviser for financial impact analysis; and, if relevant, a real estate professional familiar with retirement transitions. The expense of professional advice is a small investment compared to the cost of making the wrong decision.

Reality Check

Remember, you are choosing much more than a dwelling; you are choosing a lifestyle, a community, and a daily experience that could last potentially 30 years or more. Those holiday moments and experiences ultimately matter less than the mundane weekday afternoons. Ensure your decision is based on how you want to live, day by day, week by week, and year by year.

Your retirement home is the base for how you will live. Take time to choose this carefully. Your future self will thank you for thoughtful decision-making, and your family will benefit from seeing you thrive in a place that genuinely supports your retirement vision.

Reflection Questions for a Thriving Retirement

1. What is your vision for your retirement years?

2. How will accommodation fit into your vision?

3. What type of accommodation is essential to you; what are your minimum requirements?

4. What are the five most important factors you believe you need to discuss and seriously consider before deciding where you might end up living?

5. How important is living in an area close to medical support services (hospitals, specialists, etc.)?

6. If you're a couple, do you know what is essential to your partner for their home during retirement years?

7. If you're single, have you thought about the resources or facilities you might need to live comfortably on your own?

8. How does your housing choice align with your retirement budget and long-term financial security?

9. What are the ongoing costs (maintenance, utilities, taxes, fees, etc.) of your preferred housing option, and can you afford these on a fixed income?

10. Would downsizing free up sufficient equity that could enhance your retirement lifestyle or provide financial security?

11. How important is it to own versus rent in retirement, and what are the pros and cons of each for your situation?

12. How suitable will your preferred housing be as you age and potentially face mobility or health challenges?

13. If you plan to remain in the same place you retire to, what support services are available in your area (home care, meal delivery, transportation, etc)?

14. What's your backup plan if your current housing becomes unsuitable due to health, financial, or other changes?

15. How important is proximity to family, and how might family dynamics influence your housing decisions?

16. What recreational activities, hobbies, or interests do you want nearby, and how does your housing choice support these?

17. Do you prefer a quiet, peaceful environment or a more active, social community setting?

18. How will you build new social connections if you move to a different area or housing arrangement?

19. When is the optimal time for you to make housing changes (before retirement, early in retirement, or later)?

20. How will you test or explore potential new living arrangements before making a permanent commitment?

21. What emotional attachments do you have to your current home, and how will you process letting go if you decide to move?

22. How important are climate, weather patterns, and seasonal considerations for your daily well-being and activities?

23. Do you want to live in one location year-round, or are you interested in seasonal living arrangements?

24. What level of independence do you want to maintain, and how does your housing choice support this goal?

25. How close do you want to be to shopping, transportation, and essential services?

CHAPTER SIX

YOUR HOLIDAYS

'We've put more effort into helping folks reach retirement age than into helping them enjoy it.'

—Frank Howard Clark

What is a Holiday and Why is it Important in Your Retirement Years?

Although retirement is often expected to be a single, long holiday, it's not quite that simple. There are often still daily routines, health appointments, and similar obligations. These routines, responsibilities, and the impacts and events that often accompany ageing can mean that, even when you're retired, you may still feel stressed from time to time. Therefore, contemplating time away from home is likely worthwhile. Taking regular holidays during your retirement has the following benefits:

Physical and Mental Health: Regular travel and breaks from routine help maintain physical exercise levels, especially when holidays involve activities such as walking, swimming, or other forms of exercise. A change in environment and reduced stress can improve sleep patterns, lower blood pressure, and boost immune function.

Men-tally, holidays offer stimulation through new experiences, which is vital for cognitive health and can help prevent depression and anxiety that sometimes occur with retirement.

Social Connection and Relationship Building: Holidays often involve spending quality time with family and friends or meeting new people while travelling. This social interaction becomes increasingly important in retirement when regular workplace relationships may be missed. Group travel can strengthen existing relationships and create opportunities for new friendships with fellow travellers who share similar interests.

Personal Growth and Learning: Retirement holidays offer unique opportunities for lifelong learning and personal development. Whether exploring historical sites, learning about different cultures, trying new cuisines, or developing new skills such as photography or bird-watching, travel can satisfy intellectual curiosity and provide a sense of accomplishment and purpose.

Seasonal Flexibility and Cost Savings: Retirement offers the unique advantage of travelling during off-peak seasons when destinations are less crowded and more affordable. This flexibility allows retirees to experience popular destinations at their best while enjoying significant cost savings on flights, accommodation, and attractions. Just think of shorter queues and easier access to restaurants. I remember once queuing for three hours to ride Splash Mountain and another three hours for Big Thunder Mountain Railroad at Disney World in Orlando.

Creating Structure and Anticipation: Regular holidays help establish a framework for retirement years, offering something to look forward to and organise. This anticipation can be as rewarding as the holiday itself, such as researching projects, planning destinations, creating itineraries, and organising logistics.

Making the Most of Health and Mobility: Early retirement years often represent the optimal time for more adventurous or physically demanding travel experiences. Taking regular holidays while health and mobility are in good condition ensures enjoyable and rewarding experiences that may need to be moderated in later years.

Perspective and Gratitude: Travel experiences can provide fresh perspectives on life and cultivate gratitude for both new adventures and familiar comforts at home. This emotional benefit can contribute to overall life satisfaction and well-being during retirement.

By taking regular breaks from your routine, you help ensure that you never become stale or fall into that proverbial rut!

Despite the benefits, retirees sometimes decline to take holidays for various reasons.

My client, Jason, believed he and his wife couldn't afford it. Interestingly, even after our work together and his realisation that a holiday was affordable, he still struggled to believe he deserved one. He was one of those retirees who still believed that retirement should be an extended holiday, so he shouldn't need a holiday from his 'holiday'. It took some work to facilitate his realisation that it was something worth pursuing. Needless to say, his wife was relieved when he embraced the possibilities of special holidays.

Jason deserved holidays, and so do you. You've worked hard, and you've earned your retirement and holidays. Of course, different financial situations mean that some people can afford certain holidays while others cannot, but with planning, exploring with an open mind, and budgeting, everyone can find a chance to get a change of scenery from their everyday life. Holidays need not be expensive; options like camping in a campervan or staying in national parks are available. Not all holidays need to be overseas; in fact, there's plenty to explore in your own country: beauty, history, diversity, and culture.

If you don't consider the different experiences you want to have and plan your budget accordingly, the risk is that years will pass without intentional breaks from the retirement 'home', leading to regrets.

However, if you determine the types and nature of different holidays, plans and budgets that suit and interest you, this will likely lead to a richer and more satisfying retirement.

You'll have plenty of time in the next stage of your life. The positive challenge is contemplating how you want to spend your days, months, and years, as well as the changing seasons. Many wax lyrical about their plans to travel widely, play sports, and pursue hobbies during retirement. It's a worthwhile pursuit if you have a clear perspective. There are, however, only so many days in the year that you can live out of a suitcase, play golf, or tend to that vegetable patch in your garden.

Even if these activities of interest take up half the year, how do you intend to spend the remaining six months?

The reason for being provocative is to encourage you to intentionally plan for and live a holistic retirement filled with diverse interests, activities, experiences, and adventures.

Things to Consider While Planning Your Holidays

Before we get into tips and suggestions about how to plan your holidays, let's first discuss common concerns and considerations in relation to retirees' holidays:

Financial Constraints and Fixed Income Concerns: Many retirees worry about the cost of holidays on a fixed pension or retirement income. They often need to balance their desire to travel with concerns about depleting savings or affecting their long-term financial security. This can create anxiety about spending money on 'luxuries' such as holidays, even when they're financially feasible. However, the counter-argument to this concern is that many retirees leave considerable financial assets upon death; in other words, many never run out of money.

The statistics are quite illuminating (according to the Australian Taxation Office):

Australians inherit an average of $561,636 per person, the highest average inheritance payout worldwide. This is four times higher than the global average of $148,205. Property is the most significant component, accounting for about half of the typical estate value.

Health and Medical Considerations: Existing health conditions, mobility limitations, or medication requirements can complicate travel planning. Retirees often worry about accessing healthcare while away from home and about managing chronic conditions in unfamiliar environments. They are also concerned about whether travel insurance will adequately cover pre-existing conditions. The fear of medical emergencies abroad can be particularly concerning.

One reason travel insurance is vital is that it offers peace of mind. It's important to compare options to find the best coverage at the best price. When looking for travel insurance, specifically ask about coverage for medical evacuations, pre-existing condition waivers (often available if purchased within 14-21 days of paying an initial trip deposit), and 'cancel for any reason' policies. Think about annual policies if planning multiple trips, as they often offer better value and consistent coverage.

Additionally, holidays can take different forms. If access to adequate medical facilities is a concern, local, regional, or national holidays may be a suitable alternative to travelling overseas.

Social Dynamics and Loneliness: Widowed retirees or those whose friends have health issues may find it hard to travel alone or to find suitable travel companions. The social aspect of holidays, once shared with a spouse or close friends, might need to be rethought.

Physical Demands and Accessibility: Concerns about walking distances, stairs, bathroom facilities, and general accessibility at destinations become more prominent with age. Retirees may worry about their ability to enjoy certain types of holidays or destinations they previously loved.

Seasonal Timing and Crowds: While retirees have the flexibility to travel during off-peak periods, they may also be concerned about weather conditions, particularly if they have medical conditions affec-ted by temperature or humidity. Some are concerned about travelling during school holidays, when destinations are more crowded and expensive.

Home Security and Maintenance: Leaving home for extended periods can create anxiety about property security, garden maintenance, mail collection, and general home care. These concerns can limit the length or frequency of holidays. This ties back to the chapter on your home, where you determine what kind of dwelling will suit your lifestyle. For instance, if you plan to be a regular traveller, a townhouse may be preferable.

Technology and Booking Challenges: Some retirees feel overwhelmed by online booking systems, digital check-ins, or technology-dependent travel requirements, preferring traditional travel agents but sometimes facing higher costs or limited options.

However, embracing basic travel technology can significantly enhance your experience. Simple smartphone apps for translation, maps, currency conversion, and restaurant recommendations can provide independence and confidence while travelling. Most destinations now offer free Wi-Fi, making it easier to stay connected with family and access helpful information.

Fear of Overcommitment: After years of a structured working life, some retirees worry about overscheduling their retirement or feeling obligated to travel when they'd prefer to stay home and enjoy their newfound freedom. These adjustments all take time to work through what's best for your situation and preference. That is where planning can be very helpful, thinking about destinations and the desired frequency of travel.

Some aspects to think through and be realistic about:

- Holidays take planning. You probably shouldn't wait until the last minute to decide what you want to do. However, some of the best holiday experiences can be those that are initiated on impulse.

- Holidays can be expensive, particularly overseas in countries where the local currency is much stronger than your currency.

- You may be unable to participate in all the same types of holiday activities you once experienced.

- There can be some incredible and affordable holiday deals for retirees.

Having provided a salutary cautionary note regarding holidays, reflect on the incredible gift of being able to travel.

The above list may seem a bit disconcerting, but hopefully it hasn't dampened your enthusiasm for different types of holidays. You must be realistic throughout this process. But now that those essential considerations have been addressed, hold onto these wonderful truths as you plan for holidays:

- You have more time for holidays than you ever did when you were younger.
- Taking holidays can help keep you youthful and open-minded.
- Holidays can be an excellent way for you to form and cultivate new friendships.
- No more 'work' mental load for a job you must return to, making it easier to unwind.

Alternative Holiday Styles for Different Needs

Slow Travel and Extended Stays: Month-long stays in single destinations rather than rushed itineraries may be attractive. This approach enables deeper cultural immersion, offers potential cost savings through monthly rates, and reduces travel fatigue. It also helps you form friendships with the locals.

Multi-Generational Holidays: Travelling with adult children and grandchildren can create lifelong memories and shared experiences. Think about destinations with activities for all ages and a variety of accommodation options, like holiday rentals suitable for extended families.

Educational and Themed Travel: From photography workshops in Tuscany to cooking classes in Thailand, and from historical tours through ancient civilisations to themed travel, these experiences can be deeply satisfying. Themed travel can offer structure and deeper engagement with destinations.

Holiday Planning Ideas and Checklist Items

Depending on your personality, you may want to plan your local and overseas holidays down to the month and year or be more impulsive and free-spirited. Nevertheless, intentionality and planning are always beneficial and conducive to an enjoyable, stress-free vacation.

Whichever way you decide to approach and plan your holidays, here are some considerations and tips:

- Which season would you like to travel? Whether it's exploring vast wilderness areas, beautiful coastlines, historic cities, or tropical islands. Or mountain ranges (from the Canadian Rockies to New Zealand's fjords, from Scotland's highlands to Japan's cherry blossoms) at the time of your choosing, rather than having to shoehorn them into your annual leave!

  For those of us in the Southern Hemisphere, this often corresponds to a time of year when it's winter in Europe or North America.

  One of my clients had a real aversion to the cold but loved to travel overseas. So, he and his wife decided to time their departures from Adelaide in late May for Europe, returning in September. In that way, they escape most of the Australian winter every time they travel.

  For people in the Northern Hemisphere, this might mean escaping harsh winters for the warmth of Southeast Asia. In contrast, people in the Southern Hemisphere can enjoy European summers during their winter months.

- Setting aside an annual holiday budget as part of your living expenses is wise to prevent overspending and act as a sanity check on actual holiday costs.

  Consider implementing a tiered holiday budget system. Allocate funds for one major international trip, two to three domestic getaways, and several local day trips or weekend escapes. This approach ensures variety while effectively managing costs.

- Have you ever thought of house swapping? If you register with one of the house-swapping companies, you can request a house in one of your preferred destinations. Some companies charge an annual fee, while others offer their services free of charge. Third Home, Home Exchange and Trusted House Sitters are a few examples. In the case of Trusted House Sitters, you will be expected to look after the house, pets and/or plants. Additional options for your ongoing research:

  https://www.theguardian.com/travel/2015/dec/07/10-best-home-swap-home-sharing-websites.

- Be sure that your passport is always valid before you travel. Countries requiring six months of validity include mainland China, Mongolia, Vietnam, Cambodia, Laos, Thailand, Malaysia, Singapore, Indonesia, Burma, India, Nepal, Pakistan, Russia, Kuwait, Saudi Arabia, Bahrain, Qatar, the United Arab Emirates, Oman, Jordan, Israel, Egypt and Turkey. This list is subject to change at any time, so always check the relevant website well before you travel.

  Also, well in advance of your travel, determine whether you require a visa for your destination country.

- If you travel to the U.S.A. for less than 90 days, you will typically be required to apply for an Electronic System for Travel Authorisation. You can enter the US through the Visa Waiver Program (VWP). If you plan to travel for 90 days or more, you must apply for a visa before departure. In any case, always verify with your travel agent or online, as these conditions are subject to change occasionally. Canada has a similar system. In both instances, the approval process is highly efficient and cost-effective.

- If you have a penchant for overseas travel, it may be worthwhile to consider the type of retirement accommodation you end up tran-sitioning to. Moving to a townhouse or a unit will simplify your planning and preparation before travel. This type of living allows you to close the door and head off to the airport without worrying about gardens, security, or other concerns.

• Likewise, a fundamental consideration in this scenario is whether to have a pet. As previously mentioned, dogs are wonderful companions that help raise one's serotonin levels. However, having to find a pet sitter every time you travel may prove prohibitively expensive. Dogs can become emotionally distressed when separated from their owners, particularly after prolonged separations. Alternatively, if you have family or friends who are dog lovers, they may be willing to house and dog-sit for you or allow your pet to stay with them.

When Samantha and Miles came to see me, they were living in a large house with a swimming pool and a sizeable garden. During coaching sessions, they created a list of overseas countries they intended to visit. That list was extensive, so after deliberating for some time, they decided to sell their family home and ended up with a much smaller townhouse (with two sunny patios, minimal upkeep, and no garden).

• You may be a supporter of an overseas charity that is involved in social action or community development. Visiting and volunteering at such an organisation could be an enriching experience. You could combine this overseas trip with a holiday to a neighbouring country or one in the same region as the charity.

• Maybe you've always wanted to travel around your own country in a caravan or a motor home. Well, now is your opportunity. According to Tourism Research Australia, there are an estimated 30,000 to 40,000 grey nomads living on the road each quarter. If this is something you want to explore, check out their website: https://www.thegreynomads.com.au/

Bryn and Sue told me that they had both held busy corporate roles for most of their working lives and hadn't let their hair down, travelling off the beaten track. Most of their holidays involved flying to a resort for no more than 10 days before returning to hectic work schedules. They wanted to break free in this next stage of life and explore new adventures. They were somewhat ambivalent about hiring a campervan but were interested in exploring the option. I suggested they hire one for two to three weeks, try it, and decide whether it

 AN ABUNDANT LIFE BEYOND RETIREMENT

was a good fit. They were hooked after two weeks and ultimately made an offer on the van they had hired.

Similarly, Margaret from Toronto discovered 'slow travel' after retirement. Instead of her previous pattern of week-long European tours, she began renting apartments for month-long stays in different cities. Her first month in Prague, followed by a month in Vienna, allowed her to learn basic German, develop local friendships, and gain a genuine understanding of Central European culture, all while spending less than she would have on traditional hotel-based tours.

Additional Practical Checklist

- Travel Health Preparations: Schedule a travel medicine consultation 4-6 weeks before international travel. Update routine vaccinations and discuss destination-specific health precautions.

- Communication Plans: Set up regular check-in times with family, understand international phone and data plans, and make sure someone at home has copies of your itinerary and important documents.

- Cultural Preparation: Learn about local customs, tipping practices, and basic phrases in the local language. This preparation improves interactions and demonstrates respect for local cultures.

- International house-sitting opportunities through TrustedHouse sitters.com, Nomador, or MindMyHouse.

- Senior travel groups like ElderTreks, Road Scholar, or local senior centres often organise group travel with built-in social connections.

Holidays (no matter what form they take) are a vital consideration as you navigate your retirement years. It's a valuable opportunity to explore diverse cultures and experience different climates, languages, cuisines, histories, and other aspects of international travel. Local travel, whether interstate, intra-state, coastal or bush, will equally present a collection of many happy memories to cherish for the rest of your life.

The core idea is to be intentional about your travel goals while stay-ing flexible about how they develop. Begin with destinations and experiences you are most passionate about. Plan carefully but leave space for spontaneity. Remember that the aim is enrichment and joy, not ticking off a list. Your retirement years give you the valuable gift of time. Use it to explore, discover, and create memories that will support you for years to come.

The world is your oyster... go out and enjoy whenever and wherever you travel!

Reflection Questions for a Thriving Retirement

1. What are the holiday experiences you have most enjoyed so far?

2. How often would you like to take a holiday?

3. Could you envisage a house swap?

4. Do you have a pet? If so, how will you incorporate this into your holiday planning?

5. What are your top five local and international locations?

6. What type of holidays energises you most (adventure and exploration, relaxation, cultural immersion, or social experiences)?

7. Do you prefer independent travel where you plan everything yourself, or guided tours and organised experiences?

8. How important is luxury versus budget-conscious travel to you, and how does this align with your retirement finances?

9. What is your ideal holiday length (long weekends, week-long trips, or extended adventures)?

10. How might your physical abilities and health conditions influence your travel choices?

11. What accommodation or planning considerations do you need for any health conditions or medications?

12. Are you comfortable with long flights, or do you prefer destinations within driving distance or shorter travel times?

13. How will you access healthcare or handle medical emergencies while travelling?

14. What percentage of your retirement budget are you willing to allocate to holidays?

15. How will you balance your desire to travel with other financial priorities?

16. Are you interested in exploring more affordable travel options like off-season travel, house-sitting, or volunteer tourism?

17. Do you prefer travelling solo, with your partner, with friends, or in groups? How might this change in retirement?

18. Are you interested in meeting new people while travelling, or do you prefer more private experiences?

19. Do you want to travel during traditional holiday seasons, or take advantage of off-peak times for better prices and fewer crowds?

20. How will seasonal weather patterns influence your travel timing and destinations?

21. What do you hope to gain from your retirement travels (personal growth, education, relaxation, adventure, connection, etc.)?

22. Are you interested in travel experiences like volunteering abroad, learning new skills, or cultural exchange?

23. How might travel contribute to your overall retirement purpose and well-being?

24. What travel documents, insurance, or preparations do you need to update for retirement travel?

25. How will you stay connected with family and handle responsibilities at home while travelling?

CHAPTER SEVEN

YOUR WORK

'Retire from a job, but don't retire from making meaningful contributions.'

—Stephen Covey

'Once you take the work away, most people have no idea what to do.'

—Bryan Borzykowski

Yet this presents retirement's most significant opportunity: the chance to discover what work truly means to you when it is driven by passion rather than necessity, by purpose rather than that regular pay slip.

Work, whether paid or voluntary, has many benefits:

- Provides you with a strong sense of purpose.
- Helps to sustain your overall well-being.
- Keeps you physically active.
- Sets a positive example to future generations.
- Provides you with social interaction and potential friendships.

Let's take a moment to reflect on the value of work, its meaning, and the benefits mentioned earlier. When thinking about retirement, what are your thoughts on the nature of 'work' in this 'third stage of life'? What comes to mind?

Redefining Work Beyond the Pay Slip

For many, the word 'work' conjures images of commutes, deadlines, stress and their pay slip. But as we enter retirement, we have a rich opportunity to reimagine what work means entirely. This is about discovering what energises you, what gives your days structure, and what allows you to continue contributing meaningfully to the world around you.

The transition from a career to retirement often results in an unexpected loss of identity. 'What do you do' becomes a loaded question when your answer is no longer tied to a job title.

Whenever this topic arises with my clients, I ask them to reflect on how they would answer this question from a stranger at a dinner party: *'What do you do, or are you still working?'* The natural and often common response *is 'I'm retired'.*

However, alternatives could be:

'I am involved in a portfolio of working interests as well as various hobbies. Specifically, these work interests involve ...'

'Yes, I'm still working. I sit on two different boards, I volunteer for the local surf lifesaving club on weekends during summer, and I consult to not-for-profit organisations on change management and fundraising capabilities.'

'I'm a volunteer at three different organisations.'

'I train volunteers once a week and work in an art gallery three times a week in the mornings.'

'I operate my own consulting business on a part-time basis, and the wonderful aspect is that whenever I want to take a holiday, I simply put a sign on my email saying that I'm out of the office.'

These quotes reframe what it means to transition healthily to your next stage of working, rather than labelling yourself as retired, a word that is often perceived as pejorative.

This is precisely why rethinking work in retirement is so crucial. It's about finding purposeful engagement that aligns with who you are becoming, not just who you were.

To stimulate your thinking on what that purposeful engagement may mean for you, spend some time reflecting on these different retirement transition options:

- Cold Turkey: A hard stop from full-time work to full retirement.
- Glide Path: A gradual reduction in hours and responsibilities over 3-5 years.
- Portfolio Career: Multiple part-time roles in different areas of interest.
- Encore Career: New career in a completely different field.
- Bridge Employment: Part-time work in your current field.
- Gap Year: Taking a sabbatical for 6-12 months before deciding on long-term plans.

This is by no means an exhaustive list. However, as you reflect on the options above, you may identify additional examples that are more appropriate for your specific circumstances.

The Psychology of Purposeful Activity

Research consistently shows that people who maintain some form of meaningful work or structured activity in retirement report higher levels of life satisfaction, better cognitive function, and improved physical health. Our brains are wired to seek challenge, growth, and contribution. When we remove these elements entirely, we often experience what psychologists call 'retirement syndrome'. This can manifest in a sense of restlessness, loss of purpose, and even depression.

The paradox cuts both ways: retirement is often our first chance to pursue work we care about, freed from the need to work for money.

Without the pressure of mortgage payments and school fees, we can finally ask ourselves:

'What would I do if I didn't need the money?'

One of the questions I pose to my clients is:

'Given you might have 30 or more years in this next stage of life, how will you spend your time, what do you truly want to do, and who do you genuinely want to be?'

In most cases, I stop them before they attempt to answer the question; instead, I ask them to write down the question, reflect on it, and bring their answer to our next coaching session.

Four Dimensions of Retirement Work

1. Legacy Work

This involves sharing your accumulated wisdom, skills, and experience with others. It might mean mentoring young professionals, teaching, writing, or consulting in your field.

Legacy work says, *'I've learned something valuable, and I want to pass it on.'*

2. Discovery Work

These are the pursuits you never had time for during your full-time working years. Perhaps it's learning a new language, mastering a craft, studying art history, or delving into photography. Discovery work is about growth and curiosity. It's about realising and embracing the desire to immerse yourself in learning and discovering new things.

3. Service Work

This dimension encompasses volunteering, community involvement, and activities that contribute to causes larger than oneself. Service work provides the deep satisfaction that comes from making a difference, regardless of any financial compensation. People who are strongly 'other person-centred' tend to gravitate to service work.

4. Creative Work

Whether it's writing, painting, gardening, cooking, or any other creative pursuit, this type of work feeds the soul. Creative activities enable self-expression and often lead to 'flow states' where creativity arises naturally. When this happens, time simply disappears. That's where a person might say: *'Where on earth did today go?'*

Cultural Perspectives on Retirement Work

The concept of retirement work varies significantly across cultures. In many Asian societies, the concept of complete retirement is relatively new. Older adults in these societies have traditionally continued to contribute through family businesses or community roles. In Japan, about one in four people aged 65 and older were still working in 2022. In Europe, Sweden has the highest percentage of people aged 75 and over who are still working.

Indigenous cultures worldwide have long valued the wisdom and continued participation of elders.

In contrast, Western societies are rediscovering what many cultures never forgot: that age brings valuable perspective, not obsolescence. The Japanese have a concept called 'ikigai'. This is about finding purpose at the intersection of what you love, what you're good at, what the world needs, and what you can be paid for. It offers a framework that's particularly helpful as you deliberate on the possible nature of work in your retirement.

The Rhythm of Retirement Work

Unlike career work, work undertaken in retirement doesn't need to follow traditional patterns. You might work intensely for three months, then take a month off. You might work four hours a day instead of eight. You might combine multiple types of work (teaching in the morning, volunteering in the afternoon, and pursuing creative projects in the evening or on the weekend).

This flexibility is one of the greatest gifts that retirement can offer you. You can now create a rhythm that aligns with your natural energy patterns, seasonal preferences, and life circumstances. The key is to be intentional about this rhythm rather than simply drifting from day to day without any semblance of basic structure.

Building Your Work Portfolio

Consider developing a 'work portfolio' that combines activities to create a fulfilling and balanced retirement. This might include activities that:

- Provide intellectual stimulation.
- Offer social connection.
- Contribute to your community.
- Allow for creative expression.
- Engage in regular physical activity (sport, gym, aerobics, Pilates, etc.).

The benefit and richness of this approach is that you're not putting all your eggs into one basket. If one activity becomes less fulfilling or circumstances change, you have others to fall back on.

Embracing Digital Opportunities

The digital revolution has created unprecedented opportunities for work during your retirement. Online platforms enable teaching, consulting, writing, and creative work that can reach global audiences from the comfort of a home office.

Consider whether some of these ideas may suit you:

- Online Teaching: Platforms such as Coursera, Udemy, or Skillshare enable you to monetise decades of expertise.

- Remote Consulting: Video conferencing via Zoom, Google Meet, and Microsoft Teams enables consulting work without geographic constraints.

- Digital Creative Work: Platforms such as Etsy, Amazon KDP, and YouTube can turn creative hobbies into income streams.

- Virtual Volunteering: Organisations worldwide need remote assistance with everything from grant writing to digital marketing.

The idea is starting with platforms that match your comfort level with technology while remaining open to gradual skill development.

The Financial Dimension

Working in retirement doesn't need to be about money. Some retirees find that part-time work or casual consulting provides welcome additional income and helps their retirement savings last longer. Others discover that their unpaid retirement work saves them money by providing social connection and purpose that they might otherwise seek through expensive hobbies or travel.

The key is to separate your need for income from your need for purpose. Once you've secured your basic financial needs, you can make work decisions based on fulfilment rather than need.

Many retirees find that part-time work, which provides additional income, can significantly extend the longevity of their retirement savings while offering purpose and social connection. Often, this social connection is worth far more than the monetary value.

Overcoming Common Obstacles

While illegal in many countries, age bias exists. You can combat this by emphasising recent achievements, maintaining current skills, and networking strategically. It may be worthwhile to consider organisations that value mature workers (often nonprofits, educational institutions, and companies with age-diverse leadership).

If you are concerned about outdated skills, consider exploring different course options, online learning opportunities, or volunteering programs that offer training. Many employers value soft skills such as communication, problem-solving, reliability, etc. In this regard, experience is seen an asset.

Design work around your optimal hours and energy levels. A significant number of retirees find that they're most productive in the mornings, making consulting work or part-time positions ideal. Remote work can eliminate fatigue associated with commuting.

Starting the Conversation with Yourself

As you consider what work might look like in your retirement, ask yourself:

What activities make you lose track of time? What problems in the world concern you most? What skills do you have that others might benefit from? What have you always wanted to learn or try? What legacy do you want to leave?

These questions don't have immediate answers, and that's perfectly fine. The exploration itself is part of the journey. Some retirees spend their first year simply experimenting with different activities, treating it as a discovery phase rather than expecting immediate clarity.

The Evolution Continues

Remember that work in retirement, like retirement itself, is a journey. What energises you at 65 might be different from what fulfils you at 75. Stay open to evolution and change. The goal is to maintain an

active and engaged relationship through purposeful activities throughout your retirement years.

Your work in retirement can be one of the most rewarding aspects
of this new life stage. It's your chance to define success on your own
terms, to contribute in ways that matter to you, and to continue
growing as a person. The question to wrestle with is what work will
look like and what it will mean to you.

Work can and does take many forms, including pre-retirement and
during retirement. It can also be full-time, part-time, fixed-term,
casual, seasonal or volunteer.

You may currently be at a critical juncture in your life. It is therefore
timely to consider how much longer you want to actively engage in
the workforce and how you would like to spend your final years at
work. Or maybe you've already left full-time employment and are
considering whether you want to continue working, perhaps in a
different role or area.

Are You Ready to Leave Full-Time Employment?

I work with many clients who are looking forward to retirement but
are concerned about losing some of the benefits listed above. I also
have clients who don't want to retire because they're afraid of losing
those same benefits. In each case, I usually respond, *'You don't have
to retire just because you've reached a certain age.'*

If you are confident that you are ready to leave full-time employment,
then that is probably the right decision for you. Even if you change
your mind later, you can always look to return to work, in whatever
way it suits and works for you.

For others, leaving work 'all in one go' can be daunting and or
undesirable. In many cases, the suddenness of the change may be
a shock to the system.

Let's explore some alternatives to leaving work entirely.

The Demand for Mature Workers in Retirement

In the United States, new census data revealed that more Americans are working past the traditional retirement age of 65 than a decade ago.

Between 2014 and 2018, the share of seniors aged 65 to 74 who were employed increased to nearly 26%, up from 25.2% in the previous five-year period, according to the government's American Community Survey. The percentage of Americans aged 75 and older in the workforce also rose, to 6.6% from 5.9% over that span, according to the census.

The participation rate among Australians aged 55-64 increased from 61% in 2021 to 69.5% in 2024. However, other OECD countries perform better (e.g., New Zealand, 80.1%; Switzerland, 77.8%). There is evidence that many older Australians who would like to work are unable to do so due to age discrimination or a lack of relevant skills.

2024 Labour force participation rate 55–64-year-olds (Australia 69.5%)

% of population in same age group, 2024

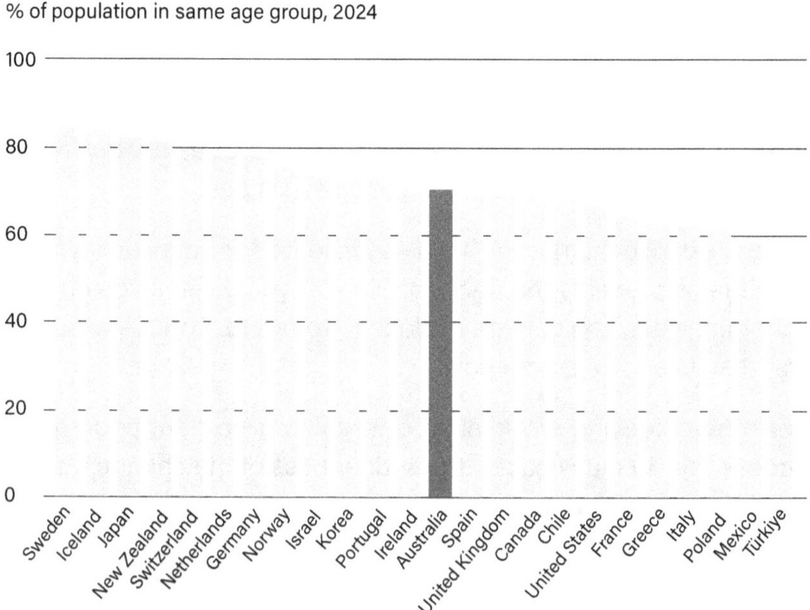

Source: 2023 OECD DATA

Countries with the highest participation rates for 55–64-year-olds often share common features:

Strong anti-age discrimination laws (like those in New Zealand and Norway), flexible work arrangements (standard in the Netherlands), and cultures that value both experience and innovation.

Some of the findings of a survey of Australian Human Resources Institute (AHRI) members (2021) in association with the Australian Human Rights Commission were as follows:

- Sixty-five per cent of the sample group expect to retire at 66 years of age or older (compared with 58 per cent in 2018).
- Twenty-six per cent expect to retire at 71 years or older (20.3 per cent in 2018).

This trend is global. In Japan, the number of workers aged 65 and above increased by 18% between 2019 and 2023. In the UK, the Office for National Statistics reports that employment rates for people aged 50-64 reached 72.1% in 2023, the highest on record. Germany's 'Rente mit 67' policy reflects similar demographic pressures, while Scandinavian countries lead in creating age-friendly workplaces.

A 2016 Stanford University report indicated that in 2012, 17% of Americans aged 70 to 74 were still working at least 10 hours per week, up from approximately 12% in 2000. The reason is that workers with higher educational attainment and higher incomes stay in the workforce longer.

In 2017, McCrindle published an infographic indicating that by 2047, Australia's population is expected to reach 36.5 million. In 1975, the ratio of workers to retirees was 7.5:1; by 2055, this is expected to change to 2.5:1, representing a significant resource challenge for Australia. Where will these additional workers come from to meet market demand? This could open work opportunities for retirees who wish to continue working in some capacity.

These facts and figures illustrate an increasing propensity for mature workers to continue working longer. Coupled with this trend, there is a corresponding demand for more people to enter and remain in the workforce.

As you approach retirement, you may consider re-entering the workforce after a refreshing holiday or a well-deserved sabbatical.

The demand for mature workers is undeniable. If you have derived rich satisfaction from your time in the workforce, you may have concluded that you still have much to contribute and are more than happy to re-engage. This employment may not necessarily be in the same sector or, indeed, the same profession (as you may have developed a wide-ranging set of skills and knowledge). It may not necessarily be in a full-time capacity. You may pursue three days instead, serving on one or two boards or some other form of part-time employment.

This may not be for everyone, but if it's something you believe would suit you, be encouraged by the growing demand for mature workers.

There is broad acceptance that ageism is rife in the developed economies. There's a saying that once you reach the age of 45, you're 'on the proverbial scrap heap' and, therefore, unemployable. I firmly believe that this form of discrimination will cease due to market demand forces, but more importantly, due to recognising the value and contribution mature workers can make to an organisation.

Several recruitment agencies currently place mature workers, and this trend is expected to increase. The global recruiter SEEK already has a section called 'Seeking Seniors'.

Flexible Work Options

Just as expectant parents have nine months to prepare and adjust to the reality of having a new person in their lives and their home, it can also be the case with retirement. Both are major inflection points in life, accompanied by a sense of loss (albeit possibly subconsciously) and followed by new beginnings. Moving one day from a relatively structured context to a situation where you have all the time to do whatever you choose is a significant adjustment. It, therefore, makes eminent sense to transition to retirement gradually.

There is no ideal time to make this transition; we're all different. However, if you are not ready to leave full-time employment, transitioning over a medium-term duration (approximately five years) can help ensure a relatively smooth change. Even if others are venturing down the 'cold turkey' route, which may not be right for you. Reflect on what works for you and be true to yourself.

You may elect to work for another five years, during which time you plan to reduce your hours. This will give you time to cultivate an existing interest, pursue a new hobby, or start a new work venture. It may also afford you more time with the grandchildren and or close friends.

One scenario is that you decrease your hours from five to four days per week and continue scaling down in prospective years:

- Year one: work four days per week.

- Year two: work three days per week.

- Year three: work two days per week.

- Year four: work one day per week and then retire.

Take some time to consider whether a flexible work arrangement might be of interest to you and suit your personality and needs. Naturally, such a decision will be contingent on whether your employer is prepared to accommodate this flexibility.

Once you've discussed this concept with your partner or confidante, meet with your employer. Be fully prepared to articulate your motivation and rationale for such a change, as well as the benefits to the organisation and yourself. More progressive companies are offering flexible working options to their employees, recognising the mutual benefits.

Australian workers are significantly interested in a gradual transition to retirement. This is evidenced in the article 'Creating a Flexible Retirement' (She's on Q), where it is mentioned that 77% of Australians surveyed who were aged 55 and older sought a flexible transition to retirement.

According to the Society for Human Resource Management's 2019 Employee Benefits survey, the share of employers offering some employees the option to phase retirement through an informal program has risen steadily in recent years.

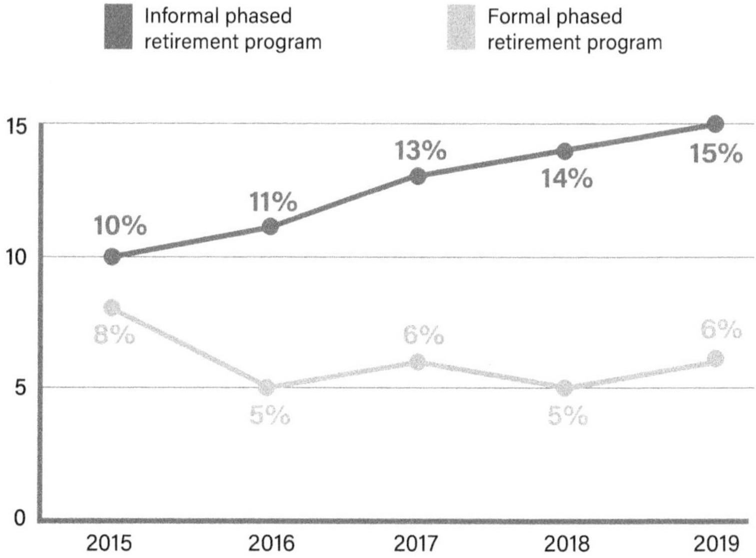

Source: Society for Human Resource Management, 2019 Employee Benefits survey.

With a massive tide of baby boomers heading towards retirement, these statistics are predicted to rise sharply. As baby boomers exit the workforce, a corresponding skills shortage is expected. This is a natural segue to the prospect of continuing to work in retirement.

Mentoring

People transitioning from full-time roles to retirement over approximately five years can give back to their workforce, community, or society through mentoring.

Mentoring in the final years of employment can significantly benefit the organisation by skilling up new and less experienced employees. It can also sustain the mentors' satisfaction and motivation during this phase of employment.

A mentor imparts their knowledge, skills, wisdom, and experience to a less experienced employee. This typically occurs through a formal structure of regular meetings within the workplace or community. There are also less-structured interventions in which meetings are less formal and occur at less frequent intervals.

These meetings are strictly confidential and therefore a safe place for the mentee to be honest, authentic, and vulnerable, where appropriate and helpful. At the outset, the mentor's role is to listen to and understand the mentee's story, experience, and developmental needs. Once completed, this naturally leads to discussing and identifying their mentoring goals. The agenda focuses on the mentee's needs, aspirations and goals.

There are many opportunities for mentoring outside of your own company. You may wish to pursue this while working or once retired. I mentor university students at my alma mater, the University of Sydney, which I find immensely satisfying. They are the leaders and innovators of tomorrow, so what better way to invest?

Think of mentoring as another way of giving back to your community and society. A philosophy of being 'other person-centred' is both healthy and positive. While you give of yourself, you also receive so much in return. Spending time in this way is both satisfying and meaningful.

Consider Elena, a former Spanish teacher from Mexico City, who discovered that her bilingual skills were in high demand for helping immigrant families navigate healthcare systems. What started as informal translation assistance evolved into consulting work with hospitals and community organisations across North America. Her work during her retirement combined her linguistic abilities, cultural understanding, and desire to serve, while providing a modest income and deep satisfaction.

In Copenhagen, retired engineer Lars transformed his woodworking hobby into a social enterprise, teaching traditional Danish furniture-making techniques to refugees while creating custom pieces for local restaurants. His workshop became a bridge between cultures, preserving craftsmanship while fostering integration.

Volunteering

A study by the Corporation for National and Community Service found that Americans over 60 who volunteered reported lower disability rates and higher well-being than those who did not.

Volunteering at any stage of life provides value to the volunteer and their community. Volunteering during retirement has many and varied benefits:

Instils a Sense of Purpose

As mentioned previously, having a clear purpose in this stage of life is strongly correlated to positive mental and physical health. If one dimension of your retirement purpose is to be other-person-centred, volunteering is one way to achieve this.

Helps Maintain and Sustain Well-Being

Supporting your community and its people provides purpose and the opportunity for social interaction, fostering a sense of connectedness, meaning, mental stimulation, and personal challenge. Therefore, this supports a positive self-image. In the medium term, it also sustains mental health and assists in lowering anxiety, loneliness, and depression.

Keeps You Physically Active

Many retirees lead sedentary lifestyles (reading, watching TV, spending too much time indoors) and fail to appreciate and realise the benefits of physical activity. It's not healthy to stay at home too long and too often. Getting out, socialising, being active, walking while volunteering, and participating in and supporting sporting activities can improve physical health.

Sets a Positive Example for Future Generations

Society is becoming self-absorbed and self-centred, which, in my view, is a very unhealthy approach to living and to life itself. Consequently, people can be prone to selfishness... *'I look after myself and am not interested in other people's needs.'* If more mature-aged people are actively engaged in their communities, it can set a positive example and inspire future generations.

International volunteering has evolved beyond traditional missionary or aid work. Consider programs such as Voluntary Service Overseas (VSO), which places skilled professionals in developing countries, and Earthwatch, which engages volunteers in scientific research worldwide. For those preferring domestic options with international impact, many local organisations support global causes (from refugee resettlement assistance to fair trade cooperatives).

Research has found that participation in voluntary services significantly predicts better mental and physical health, life satisfaction, self-esteem, happiness, lower depressive symptoms, psychological distress, mortality and functional inability.

In 'How to Live Better in 2025: The Power of Giving', David Robson cites several research studies at various reputable universities that attest to these positive effects on physical and mental health. One example was a longitudinal study conducted by the University of Wisconsin-Madison. Ten thousand high school leavers were asked to provide information about different types of organisations they were involved in as volunteers (e.g., Rotary, school boards, not-for-profit organisations, aid organisations, community groups, sports clubs, social welfare societies).

They found that people who regularly volunteered for such organisations reported experiencing better physical and mental health over time. Specifically, their sense of well-being increased after they started volunteering. If they volunteered at two or more organisations, they benefited more than people who volunteered at one or none. The longer they volunteered, the greater the benefit realised, compared to people who had just started volunteering.

Testing the Waters of Work

As you consider where and how to begin, a 'try before you buy' approach may be a wise choice. It can prevent potential disappointment or frustration before you become too involved. A couple of different approaches for you to consider:

The 90-Day Exploration Plan:

- Days 1-30: Shadow or interview people doing work that interests you.

- Days 31-60: Volunteer or take on small projects in potential areas.

- Days 61-90: Begin formal applications, proposals, or commitments based on your experiences.

The Portfolio Approach Timeline:

- Year 1: Focus on one primary activity while exploring others.

- Year 2: Add a second dimension once the first is established.

- Year 3 plus: Fine-tune your portfolio based on what energises you most.

If you embark on either of these approaches iteratively, it will be healthy to review and ask these questions:

- Do you look forward to your work activities?

- Are you learning and growing?

- Do you feel you're making a meaningful contribution?

- Are you maintaining social connections?

- Does your work complement rather than overwhelm your retirement lifestyle?

Utilising this rigorous approach in future work opportunities will ultimately lead to well-informed decisions.

It stands to reason that if we are engaged in our community, relating to people, supporting them, and contributing to meritorious causes (for altruistic reasons), we will be better off than staying at home all day. Keeping active and moving around in our world is a positive distraction from any worries or frustrations we may experience at home or in life. The motto is to keep moving and active for as long as possible.

Retire from a job, but don't retire from making meaningful contributions. Work, in and of itself, is a gift and a significant contributor to a healthy sense of well-being. Work, even in retirement, is beneficial. The beauty is that when you retire, you have a plethora of work options to choose from.

The Oxford Dictionary defines work as an activity involving mental or physical effort to achieve a purpose or result. This could mean many different things to various individuals. The principle to grasp, internalise and act on is that this form of participation creates purpose and value not only for you but also for your community.

Remember that work during retirement is generally iterative rather than permanent. You might spend two years consulting, three years volunteering intensively, then shift to creative pursuits or community leadership. This evolution reflects retirement's greatest gift: the freedom to redefine success, contribution, and fulfilment on your terms.

Your accumulated wisdom, skills, and life experience represent decades of valuable human capital. The choice is yours on how you share your gifts with the world. Whether through paid work, volunteering, mentoring, or creative expression, your continued engagement enriches not only your retirement but the communities fortunate enough to benefit from your experience.

Reflection Questions for a Thriving Retirement

1. At this stage, when do you think you may want to retire from your organisation or business?

   - In 0-2 years: _______________
   - In 2–4 years: _______________
   - In 3–5 years: _______________
   - In 5 plus years: _______________

2. If afforded the opportunity, would you explore the prospect of becoming a mentor at your organisation? (Appreciating your significant organisational experience and knowledge, you may be interested in supporting a less experienced employee).

3. What are your thoughts and interests regarding part-time or casual work in retirement, possibly in an area unrelated to what you currently do?

4. Does volunteering locally, interstate or overseas appeal to you? If yes, what research have you undertaken in this area?

5. What aspects of your current work give you the most satisfaction and energy? How could you incorporate these elements into retirement work?

6. Are you interested in working in retirement primarily for financial reasons, social connection, sense of purpose, or personal fulfilment?

7. What would need to be different about work in retirement compared to your current career for it to feel rewarding rather than burdensome?

8. How will you know when you are truly ready to stop working entirely?

9. What unique skills, knowledge, or expertise do you have that could benefit others in retirement?

10. Are you interested in teaching, training, or consulting in your field of expertise?

11. What new skills would you like to develop that could open up different work opportunities in retirement?

12. How could you package your experience into speaking, writing, or advisory roles?

13. What's your ideal work schedule in retirement (seasonal work, project-based assignments, or regular part-time hours)?

14. How important is workplace flexibility, remote work options, or the ability to travel while working?

15. Would you prefer working independently as a consultant/ freelancer or being part of an organisation or team?

16. What boundaries do you want to set around work commitments to protect your retirement lifestyle?

17. How could you begin testing retirement work options while still in your current career?

18. What networks from your career could support your retirement work goals?

19. Are there ways to gradually reduce your current work responsibilities while taking on new, more fulfilling roles?

20. How will you handle the potential income reduction that might come with retirement work?

21. What kind of impact do you want your retirement work to have on others or your community?

22. Are you interested in working with specific populations (youth, seniors, disadvantaged communities, etc.)?

23. How does your potential retirement work align with your overall purpose and values?

24. What training, certifications, or credentials might you need for your desired retirement work?

25. How will retirement work affect your taxes, benefits, or pension arrangements?

26. What is your backup plan if your first choice for retirement work doesn't work out as expected?

27. How will you balance work commitments with other retirement priorities like travel, family time, or personal interests?

28. What causes or organisations align most closely with your values and interests?

29. Do you prefer hands-on volunteer work or behind-the-scenes administrative support?

30. How much time are you willing to commit to volunteer activities, and how will this fit with other retirement plans?

31. What skills do you want to use in volunteering, and what new experiences do you want to gain?

CHAPTER EIGHT

YOUR INTERESTS AND HOBBIES

'A hobby a day keeps the doldrums away.'

—Phyllis McGinley

'Engaging in hobbies and interests in retirement keeps the mind sharp, the heart full, and the spirit young.'

—Unknown

In our working lives, we never have as much time as we'd like to pursue our hobbies and interests. Now, in your retirement years, you can finally explore new activities or dedicate time to a hobby or interest you already love.

While hobbies and interests have similarities, they are distinct. Hobbies are activities we enjoy and pursue regularly, such as sports, reading, cooking, photography, and arts and crafts. There can be a grey area with hobbies because it depends on your motivation. For example, if you run, do you do it solely for health reasons or because you genuinely enjoy running?

Interests are areas we aspire to explore, learn more about, and deepen our understanding and appreciation for. Sometimes, interests can later evolve into hobbies as we transition from researching and learning about a particular area to becoming actively involved.

For instance, my client, Alexis, was seeking to learn about numismatics (the study of coins, banknotes, and medals). Over time, she developed a collection of coins from various countries, and her interest has now evolved into a hobby.

Similarly, Hans, a retired engineer, became captivated by medieval architecture during his travels. This interest led him to join heritage preservation groups, learn traditional stone-masonry techniques, and eventually volunteer on UNESCO World Heritage Site Restoration Projects across Europe. His intellectual curiosity culminated in a meaningful, hands-on contribution.

The beauty of retirement is that you now have the freedom to pursue interests without the pressure of monetisation or career progression. A hobby can remain purely for personal enjoyment, or it can develop into something more, such as teaching others, competing, or even earning a small income. The choice is completely up to you.

Do You Need a Hobby?

Failing to develop hobbies and interests, or having none, may lead to stagnation, boredom, and isolation, and to an increased risk of mortality in retirement.

You may relate to this scenario: You were busy working before retirement, consolidating your career, climbing the corporate ladder, building your own business, etc., and providing for your family. You worked long hours, including some Saturdays. The rest of the weekend was spent relaxing and involved in family activities. You had varied interests but rarely had the time, mental space or energy to pursue them. You realise that you are out of practice pursuing the interests and hobbies that are part of your character.

All is not lost; it's never too late to rekindle some of those interests and hobbies and to explore and establish new ones.

Global Perspectives on Retirement Hobbies

Different cultures approach retirement hobbies in unique ways. In Japan, many retirees engage in 'ikebana' (flower arranging) or 'bonsai' cultivation, activities that combine creativity, mindfulness, and a connection to nature. Scandinavian countries popularise 'friluftsliv' (outdoor life), hiking, cross-country skiing, and foraging, which keep retirees active all year-round.

Mediterranean retirees often centre hobbies around food culture, from winemaking in Italy to olive cultivation in Greece. In many Latin American countries, community-based activities such as dancing, music groups, and storytelling circles foster strong social connections while preserving cultural traditions.

Benefits of Having a Hobby

Findings suggest that hobbies and a sense of purpose in life may be associated with more extended longevity and greater healthy life expectancy among community-dwelling older adults.

A research article: 'Relationship of Having Hobbies and a Purpose in Life with Mortality, Activities of Daily Living, and Instrumental Activities of Daily Living Among Community-Dwelling Elderly Adults' described a longitudinal study of 4,269 residents 65 and over, which resulted in the following:

- Having neither hobbies nor Purpose in Life (PIL) was associated with an increased risk of mortality and a decline in 'daily activities of living' compared to having both hobbies and PIL.

- Findings suggest that hobbies and PIL may extend longevity and healthy life expectancy among community-dwelling older adults.

As mentioned, a hobby is an activity that a person pursues regularly. The regularity of the activity suggests that hobbies provide satisfaction, challenge, enjoyment and often a sense of joy and accomplishment. Certain hobbies involve time spent with small or large groups of people, engaging in physical activity, or in situations that involve mental challenges (e.g., crosswords, research, chess, poetry, writing).

Think of the well-being benefits of such activities:

- Physical: following participation in exercise (e.g., cardiovascular benefits).
- Emotional: the elation, satisfaction, and inspiration from achieving something.
- Psychological: the cognitive strengthening from exercising the brain and stimulating intellectual capacity.

The Centre for Cognitive Health (TCCH) (2019), in an article titled 'Hobbies, Are They Really That Important?', cited research findings showing that art therapy can enhance attention, interest, joy, self-respect, and quality of life in people with dementia.

Furthermore, the TCCH article cites the National Institute on Ageing, which found that individuals who engage in creative activities can enhance their creativity, memory, and problem-solving skills.

Professor T.F. Hughes studied the impact of hobbies on people's lives. Her findings suggested that engaging in a hobby for one or more hours each day may protect against dementia later in life.

In the article 'How Hobbies Impact Your Head and Your Heart,' (Srini Pillay M.D.), Sarah Pressman found that hobbies also result in physiological benefits. Pleasurable activities lead to lower blood pressure, lower BMI, less depression, and other positive physical benefits.

The MacArthur Study of Successful Aging, which followed nearly 1,200 older adults, found that those engaged in productive activities, including hobbies, were more likely to maintain cognitive function and physical health longer. Specifically, participants who engaged in complex hobbies requiring multiple skills (such as quilting, which involves planning, problem-solving, and fine motor coordination) had a 30-50% lower risk of developing dementia.

Additionally, research published in the American Journal of Public Health found that adults who participated in cultural activities like visiting museums, attending concerts, or engaging in arts and crafts had a 31% lower risk of developing depression over four years.

It seems logical that having different hobbies will provide holistic benefits as we age. Therefore, consider hobbies that include:

- The involvement of and interaction with people

- Some form of exercise

- Mentally challenging activities, and

- Something that utilises the right side of the brain (music, arts, crafts, etc.)

Some hobbies will naturally involve more than one of the above benefits. For example, playing bridge offers mental and social benefits, while tennis involves physical activity and interaction with others.

Addressing Retirement Hobby Challenges

Financial Concerns: Many retirees worry about the cost of new hobbies. However, most activities are eminently affordable. Libraries offer free classes, community colleges provide senior discounts, and many clubs welcome beginners by providing equipment they can loan. Consider starting with low-cost versions before investing in expensive clothing or equipment.

Physical Limitations: Age-related changes shouldn't prevent you from enjoying beloved activities. Many hobbies can be adapted for people with mobility impairments, such as seated gardening, large-print books, ergonomic craft tools, and water-based exercises. Focus on what you can do rather than what you can't.

Learning Anxiety: *I'm too old to learn new things* is a typical concern. Research consistently shows that the adult brain remains remarkably plastic. Start with activities that build on your existing knowledge, join beginner-friendly groups, or find patient mentors who enjoy teaching.

Social Hesitation: You might find that joining new groups where you are the stranger in the room triggers social anxiety within you. Many organisations have newcomer programs or buddy systems. Think about starting with short-term classes or one-off events before committing to long-term membership.

What Hobbies Would You Like to Pursue in Retirement?

What are your current hobbies and interests? Do they incorporate the social, physical, mental, and creative elements? Consider which hobbies and interests may be worth pursuing in the short term.

Some ideas:

PHYSICAL	SOCIAL
Tennis	Societies
Gardening	Club memberships
Golf	Volunteering
Cycling	Travel tours
Walking	Dinner parties
Mountaineering	Theatre
Swimming	Public speaking
MENTAL	CREATIVE
Crosswords	Painting/Drawing
Chess	Calligraphy
Adult Learning	Sculpture
Writing	Dance
Bridge	Pottery
Poetry	Gardening
Other board games	Design

Building Diverse Hobbies

Rather than choosing hobbies randomly, consider creating a balanced portfolio that addresses different aspects of well-being. Some options for consideration:

The Four-Pillar Approach

- Physical Pillar: Activities that keep your body moving and strong.
- Social Pillar: Hobbies that connect you with others and build community.
- Mental Pillar: Challenges that exercise cognitive function and learning.
- Creative Pillar: Expressions that allow personal expression.

Sample Balanced Portfolios:

- The Active Retiree: Tennis (physical and social), photography (mental and creative), book club (social and mental), cooking (creative and social)
- The Contemplative Retiree: Walking (physical), writing (mental and creative), meditation (social), birdwatching (mental and physical)
- The Community Builder: Volunteering (social), gardening (physical and creative), local history research (mental), teaching and facilitation (social and mental)

Consider these budget-friendly starting points:

- Writing: Free (just pen and paper or computer).
- Walking groups: Cost of comfortable shoes.
- Library volunteering: Free, plus social benefits.
- Community gardening: Shared costs, shared harvest.
- Online learning: Many free options available.

Digital Hobbies

Today's retirees have access to hobby opportunities that previous generations could not have imagined:

- Online Learning Communities: Platforms like MasterClass, Skillshare, or YouTube University offer world-class instruction in a wide range of subjects, from photography to philosophy.

- Virtual Travel and Exploration: Google Earth adventures, virtual museum tours, and online archaeological digs can satisfy intellectual curiosity.

- Digital Creation: Podcasting, blogging, vlogging, digital photography, or creating family history documentaries.

- Global Connections: Online chess clubs, international pen-pal programs, or virtual book clubs connecting readers worldwide.

The key is selecting technology that enhances your hobby experience.

Evolving Your Hobbies Over Time

Your hobby interests and capabilities will likely change throughout retirement. Someone might start retirement with active hiking and photography, transition to indoor photography and editing as mobility changes, then evolve into teaching photography or curating exhibitions.

How this could look at different points in retirement:

- High-energy hobbies for early retirement when physical capabilities are strongest.

- Skill-building activities that can be adapted as circumstances change.

- Teaching or mentoring opportunities that leverage accumulated expertise.

- Legacy activities like writing memoirs, creating family history projects, or documenting traditional skills.

Community Building Through Hobbies

Hobbies often foster natural communities. Photography clubs organise group outings, book clubs discuss literature over coffee, and gardening groups share seeds and advice. These communities usually go beyond the hobby itself, offering friendship, mutual support, and shared experiences that greatly enrich retirement life.

Reflect on how your hobbies could help meet wider community needs. Master gardeners teach sustainable practices, experienced woodworkers' mentor young apprentices, and avid readers often volunteer with literacy programs.

Your hobbies and interests in retirement can become some of your life's most significant sources of joy, learning, and connection. They provide structure without rigidity, challenge without constant pressure, and the opportunity to engage with a community without obligation. Whether you're rediscovering childhood passions, exploring interests you never had time for, or discovering entirely new fascinations, your hobbies are a vital part of your life and well-being.

Remember that hobbies are meant to and can enrich your life, not complicate it. Choose activities that resonate with your authentic interests, align with your current circumstances, and allow room for growth and change. Think of all the new things you can learn and enjoy, at your own pace.

Reflection Questions for a Thriving Retirement

1. What hobbies and interests did you enjoy as a teenager, young adult and later in life?

2. How many hobbies and interests could you still physically pursue, and which ones do you want to engage in actively?

3. What hobbies and interests have you always been interested in but never had the time or the motivation to pursue?

4. What are examples of healthy hobbies and interests for you to consider in retirement?

5. Could you participate in hobbies and or interests with a family member or friend?

6. When will you start researching hobbies and interests, and when will you start them?

7. What activities make you lose track of time because you're so engaged and absorbed?

8. When you browse online, visit bookstores, or scroll through social media, what topics consistently capture your attention?

9. What skills or talents do you have that you have never fully developed or explored?

10. If you could spend a day shadowing someone in any hobby or field of interest, what would you choose?

11. Do you prefer hobbies that challenge you intellectually, physically, creatively, or socially?

12. Are you drawn to activities where you can see progress and improvement over time?

13. What new skills would make you feel proud to master in your retirement years?

14. How comfortable are you with being a beginner again, and what hobbies might require this mindset?

15. Do you prefer solitary hobbies for personal reflection or group activities for social connection?

16. What local clubs, groups, or communities could you join related to your interests?

17. Are you interested in hobbies where you could teach or mentor others?

18. How could your hobbies help you build new friendships and social networks?

19. What is your budget for hobby-related expenses (equipment, classes, materials, travel)?

20. Do you have adequate space at home for your preferred hobbies, or would you need to use community facilities?

21. How will seasonal changes or weather affect your ability to pursue outdoor interests?

22. What hobbies could you pursue regardless of your future health or mobility limitations?

23. How many different hobbies do you want to pursue, and how will you balance them?

24. What mix of indoor/outdoor, social/solitary activities appeals to you?

25. Are you interested in hobbies that could potentially generate income (e.g. painting), or do you prefer purely recreational pursuits?

26. How will you prevent hobbies from becoming obligations rather than activities you enjoy?

27. Are there hobbies that could contribute to your community or help others (teaching, volunteering, creating)?

28. Could any of your interests lead to creating something lasting (art, writing, crafts)?

29. How might your hobby interests need to evolve as you age or face different life circumstances?

30. Are there 'bucket list' hobby experiences you want to pursue early in retirement, while you are most physically able?

31. How could your hobbies complement your other retirement goals (fitness, social connection, learning, travel)?

32. What hobbies might you be able to combine with travel or visiting family?

33. How will you protect time for hobbies while balancing other retirement commitments and responsibilities?

CHAPTER NINE

YOUR FAMILY AND FRIENDS

'I've had all the fame... travelled to so many countries and exotic places, rubbed shoulders with famous people, and experienced significant wealth... but I realise that family and those few very close friends are most important and what really matters.'

—David Bowie

I am a very tall person, just under two metres (my son Thomas is over two metres). As a young teen navigating puberty, I experienced a significant growth spurt, which led to the onset of endogenous depression (a type of depression caused mainly by internal factors like genetics or biochemical imbalances, rather than external stressors). During this time, I had severe bouts of melancholy, retreated from others, and missed out on forming several healthy friendships. Although I sometimes felt inadequate to make friends, I deeply yearned for a healthy-sized group of people I could call my 'mates'.

I believe we all have an innate need and desire to have a group of people we hang out with and call our friends. That is one of life's essential needs that we should all strive to realise.

Friends and Family

So, what is a friend? I am happy to say that I overcame the depressive episodes upon finishing my schooling, and over the years, I have formed and cultivated many rich and diverse friendships both inside and outside of work. But what truly makes a friend?

To me, the hallmarks of a true friend are:

- Perhaps most importantly, being with a true friend feels natural and comfortable. You can be your authentic self without fear of judgment, and their presence brings joy and meaning to your life rather than stress or drama.

- When you catch up, you walk away feeling it was time well spent, a feeling of contentedness and sometimes great encouragement.

- You know you can share deep things when it feels right to, in the knowledge that when you do, you will receive wise counsel and empathy in return.

- You have each other's backs and can depend upon each other for support.

- If you were ever in a crisis (apart from family), your close friends are the people you would turn to, because of the deep trust you have in them.

- Every now and then, you share honest truths that might be hard to hear, but you know they come from genuine care and are expressed constructively.

The Power of Appropriate Vulnerability in Building Connections

One of the most powerful tools for deepening friendships, yet one that many people struggle with, is the art of expressing vulnerability thoughtfully and appropriately. This doesn't mean overwhelming new acquaintances with a catharsis or your deepest, darkest problems, but instead, being genuinely human in your interactions.

Appropriate vulnerability might include:

- Sharing a challenge you're facing (*'I am finding retirement adjustment harder than I expected'*).

- Admitting when you don't know something (*'I have never tried this before, but I'm excited to learn'*).

- Expressing authentic emotions (*'I was moved by that story you shared'*).

- Acknowledging mistakes or uncertainties (*'I realise I may have misjudged that situation'*).

The key is reciprocal vulnerability: gradually matching the level of openness the other person demonstrates. This fosters trust, transforming acquaintances into genuine friends. Life experience often makes retirees more willing to be vulnerable than they were when maintaining professional personas.

So, what about family?

A family is a group of two or more persons related by birth, marriage, or adoption who live together for an extended period. Families can be complex, dysfunctional and challenging. They can also be places where laughter abounds, special memories are forged, and a sense of connectedness, safety, belonging, and love is felt. In well-functioning family units, they are also places where mutual trust and support are present. Parents often describe an unconditional love for their children, and in many cases, that love is reciprocated.

What resonates in these descriptions of friends and family is the enduring affection and trust. Friends enjoy each other's company;

they have a mature rapport in which self-deprecating humour is both expressed and received without defensiveness or offence. There are an unexplained kinship and a strong bond in which silence is not awkward, and mutual understanding exists on many levels.

Friends have quite a different relational bond than family. Trust forms an integral component of any mature friendship. There are things that you would discuss with friends but not necessarily with your family, and vice versa. Equally, there are perhaps emotions you would freely express or manifest with your family but not with your friends.

The family home or unit is also a place of shelter and security. Australian parents sometimes colloquially refer to their young adult children as 'boomerang kids' as they return home after living away for a while. When they come back, it may be for different reasons, but they do so because they feel comfortable and safe in their home with their family. The bond of family can be very strong. The children may also enjoy the benefits of home-cooked meals, as well as washing and ironing, which they missed while living away from home!

In some families, siblings and their parents are very close-knit, and members feel comfortable sharing the most intimate details, burdens, and emotional highs and lows. So, families can play a significant role in the well-being of each family member.

What Happens to Friendships When You Stop Working?

Some people's core group of friends comes from the people they work with, and that bond can wane and become challenging when they retire. This can be addressed if they consciously and proactively seek new friends.

The average person spends approximately 2,000 hours per year in a work environment, often including daily interactions with one or many people. A sample of some of the things people are exposed to and experience during interactions with people in the workplace (wherever that might be):

- Mental stimulation
- Humour
- Debate
- Provocation
- Encouragement
- Conflict
- Challenge
- Affirmation
- Validation
- Inspiration
- Meaningful conversations
- Practical Support
- Friendship
- Camaraderie

Research indicates that men and women often experience and maintain friendships differently. For many men, work can play a central role in daily life, leaving limited time and energy for developing or maintaining friendships outside the workplace. Social interactions among men frequently occur around shared activities, such as sports or hobbies. Women, on average, tend to form connections through conversation and relational engagement. These are general patterns rather than universal traits, and individual experiences can vary widely.

I remember speaking to the founder of a global organisation who had recently retired. He said:

'During my working life, I spent so much time on a plane and in different countries that I never really saw much of my friends. On weekends, when I was home, I spent time with my family, so I never invested in friendships. I realise now that I don't have any real friends.'

I thought to myself, 'How sad and tragic'... I ruminated about whether this was an everyday reality.

Friends and family play a crucial role in one's sense of connection and overall well-being. If anything, they become even more critical in retirement when work and possibly other activities disappear or diminish. As we age, some of our older friends (and younger ones, too, if tragedy befalls them) may no longer be around. Losing friends is a reality; cultivating new friends along life's journey is even more critical.

No one is an island; we are all wired to be relational beings who thrive on connecting with others. Whether we are introverted or extroverted, we all need and benefit from the company of others, even if we don't consciously recognise this.

Despite the deleterious impact of COVID on social interaction, it is self-evident that there are numerous benefits to interacting with people at work.

When people shift from traditional working life, they find they have significantly more free time without the routine that work provides. They also lose daily interactions with work colleagues (and customers/clients), which can often be very meaningful and mentally stimulating.

It stands to reason that friends and family may become more critical at this stage of life, given the loss of social interaction in the workplace.

Friendships in Different Cultures

Different cultures approach retirement friendships uniquely. In many Mediterranean countries, the concept of the 'piazza', the town square where people gather daily, provides natural opportunities for social engagement. Scandinavian countries often organise formal 'friendship circles' or hobby groups specifically for retirees.

In Japan, many retirees join 'silver human resources centres' that combine light work with social connection. Latin American cultures often centre retirement social life around extended family networks and neighbourhood relationships that span generations.

Consider which aspects of these cultural approaches might work in your context, such as regular gathering places, structured social activities, or intergenerational connections.

What Are the Risks of Loneliness and Social Isolation in Retirement?

As mentioned earlier, when I was a young teenager, I experienced loneliness and isolation at different times. It was during this time that I discovered American soul singer Paul Williams, whose lyric writing I admired. One of his songs, 'Loneliness', poetically captures the experience of loneliness. An excerpt of the lyrics:

Loneliness

Takes the romance out of falling stars

Fills the wishing wells and fills the bars

Run and hide the scars of loneliness

Makes the winter's night seem twice as long

Makes the summer sunlight much too strong

Nothing's really wrong

It's only loneliness

Waits in silence while the shadows grow

Waits and wonders if it's finally time to go

The yes in our hello said no to

Loneliness

The risks of loneliness and isolation in retirement are profound and far-reaching, affecting both physical and mental health in ways that can significantly impact quality of life and longevity.

The World Health Organisation now recognises loneliness as a global health epidemic comparable to smoking 15 cigarettes daily. However, research from Harvard's Grant Study, which followed subjects for over 80 years, found that good relationships not only make us happier but also keep us healthier and help us live longer.

Specific findings show that socially connected people have:

- 50% lower risk of dementia
- Reduced inflammation markers

- Better immune function
- Lower rates of depression and anxiety
- Improved sleep quality
- Faster recovery from illness

The protective effect is so strong that maintaining healthy social ties boosts survival chances, making friendship a matter of life and death.

Physical Health Consequences

Loneliness and social isolation are linked to serious health problems such as cognitive decline, depression, and heart disease. The research shows that lonely or isolated older adults are at greater risk for all-cause mortality, with individuals having strong social ties showing a much greater likelihood of survival. This mortality risk is comparable to smoking or obesity, making social connection a critical health factor.

Mental Health Impact

Feelings of social isolation and lack of companionship are reported by more than seven in ten older adults with fair or poor mental health. Depression, anxiety, and cognitive decline are common consequences of prolonged loneliness. The isolation can create a vicious cycle where mental health deteriorates, making it even harder to reach out and form connections.

The Scope of the Problem

The statistics are sobering: 50% of individuals aged over 60 are at risk of social isolation, and one-third will experience some degree of loneliness later in life. Post the COVID pandemic, more than one-third of people age 50 to 80 feel lonely, and nearly as many feel isolated.

Why Retirement Increases Risk

Retirement often removes the natural social structure that work provides. Daily interactions with colleagues, shared purposes, and regular routines disappear. Additionally, ageing brings other isolating factors like mobility limitations, loss of driving privileges, deaths of friends and family members, and potential health issues that make socialising more difficult.

The Immune System Connection

Chronic loneliness triggers stress responses that weaken the immune system, increase inflammation, and elevate cortisol levels. This makes older adults more susceptible to infections, slower to heal from injuries, and more likely to develop chronic conditions like cardiovascular disease and diabetes.

Cognitive Decline

Social interaction stimulates cognitive function through conversation, shared problem-solving, and emotional engagement. Without these regular mental exercises, cognitive decline can accelerate, potentially increasing the risk of dementia and other neurological conditions.

The good news is that there are ways to counteract these adverse effects. Maintaining social connections, joining communities, volunteering, and staying actively engaged with others can significantly reduce these health risks and improve overall well-being in retirement.

Paul Williams also sums up the purpose of friends in this song from his album 'Here Comes Inspiration':

That's What Friends Are For
Friends are like music
Sometimes, they're sad
Sometimes, they're lonely
And need to be told that they're loved.

Friends are like good wine
And I've had the best.
Don't always show it
But no one knows better than I.

Friends are like warm clothes
In the night air.
Best when they're old
And we miss them the most when they're gone.

Friends love your good side
And live with your bad.
Want you and need you
When no one else knows you're alive.

Establishing, nurturing, and sustaining friendships requires commitment, effort, and discipline. Being proactive about socialising with our friends and family is also essential. Not everyone is good at initiating, so we must be prepared and comfortable to assume that role with certain friends and family.

Being vulnerable can be a robust connector, but it also takes courage. Being open and honest, without being overly emotional, with someone you've recently met can help build trust and a fruitful friendship.

Being Aware of How Friendships Can Change and End

In life's journey, I have discovered that there are friends for different seasons. Some friends stay forever (e.g., old schoolmates). In contrast, others become friends through where we worked, studied, lived, played sports, or met via community engagement (Rotary, Lions, church, synagogue, temple, bridge, book club, etc.).

When our circumstances change, such as leaving a company, moving to a different suburb, city, or country, or changing community/sporting clubs, there's a propensity or risk of drifting away from friends.

Considering potential changes in circumstances upon retirement, which friendships might change? How could you foster new friendships?

Understanding Your Friendship Ecosystem

Rather than rigidly categorising friends, it's helpful to recognise that relationships naturally exist at different levels of intimacy and serve various purposes in our lives.

This awareness helps you:

- Recognise relationship transitions. Work friendships may deepen or fade after retirement.
- Appreciate diverse connections. Not every friend needs to be a confidante.
- Set realistic expectations. Different relationships fulfil different needs.
- Identify friendship gaps in your friendship ecosystem and consider where it would be beneficial to cultivate new friendships.

You might realise that you would benefit from a few more close friends or activity partners.

The goal is to ensure you have a balanced network of friends that provide emotional support, companionship, shared activities, and casual social interaction.

As you retire, be aware of the different friendship roles. You will benefit from investing time in maintaining and nurturing these friendships as you get older.

Suzanne Degges-White developed a list of the 13 Essential Traits of Good Friends. If you find it challenging to initiate and sustain friendships, review this list of friendship traits.

Recognise your strengths, draw on them when meeting new people, and reconnect with those you have lost touch with. In addition, reflect on the top three areas you find challenging.

Set personal development goals for each area, find someone to support and hold you accountable, and encourage you along the way.

The 13 Essential Friendship Traits:

1. I am trustworthy.
2. I am honest with others.
3. I am generally very dependable.
4. I am loyal to the people I care about.
5. I am easily able to trust others.
6. I experience and express empathy for others.
7. I can be non-judgmental.
8. I am a good listener.
9. I am supportive of others in their good times.
10. I am supportive of others in their bad times.
11. I am self-confident.
12. I am usually able to see the humour in life.
13. I am fun to be around.

Some of these areas may be challenging for you. If they are important to you and you are motivated to develop them further, consider asking a close friend to be that source of counsel and encouragement to you. You may also consider engaging a Retirement Coach to support you in these areas.

Your time in retirement allows you to reconnect with your family of origin (siblings, cousins, etc.) that you may have lost contact with for various reasons. It's also an opportunity to spend quality time with your adult children (if applicable). You no doubt recognise the truth that you never stop being a parent! This is a time and stage to deepen these relationships. You may also have (or perhaps soon) grandchildren in your life, which affords you rich experiences and a mutually beneficial growing bond.

If you have a partner for life, you have the time to do more things together and continue life's adventures together. A time to grow in your love and support for one another, and hopefully you won't feel the need to live in each other's pockets!

Reimagining Family Relationships in Retirement

Retirement offers unique opportunities to deepen family connections in various ways:

- Adult Children: Your relationship can evolve from parent-child to adult-adult friendship. This requires letting go of parental control while offering wisdom when requested. Many retirees discover that their adult children become some of their most cherished companions.

- Grandchildren: These relationships offer joy without the primary responsibility of parenting. You can be a fun, patient presence, with time for stories, games, and adventures.

- Siblings and Extended Family: Retirement often offers time to reconnect with family members you may have lost touch with during the busy years of your career. These relationships carry shared history and can become increasingly precious.

- Intergenerational Friendship: Consider befriending people of different ages. Younger friends can keep you energised, while peer relationships provide understanding of shared life experiences. Older generations provide wisdom, grit, inspiration and perspective.

On Grandparenting: Managing the Inevitable Transition

How many times have you heard friends talk about how excited they are for the arrival of their first grandchild?

Reaching the stage where one of your children is about to start their own family, just as you did, is a significant milestone. The arrival of your first grandchild is an incredibly exciting time to look forward to.

After your first grandchild's arrival, you spend years bonding and building a treasured relationship. You babysit for hours, sometimes days and nights. You take your grandchild on many outings, which keeps you young and vibrant. Family holidays with a growing family are something that you look forward to, knowing you will build special memories with your grandchild. You love reading those stories, and as they mature, you take pride in mentoring them.

Then, all too quickly, your grandchild becomes a teenager. They still love you, but they have a growing circle of friends and activities after school and on the weekends. As they mature, independence becomes vital to them. The gap between visits widens, and phone chats and texts start to wane. You miss the regularity of seeing your grandchild, sometimes even wondering whether they miss you. Slowly, it dawns on you that they have their own life. You will still be a part of it, but from the sidelines.

We were on holiday recently and got chatting with a very interesting, adventurous couple. They said that they were very invested in their grandchildren's lives and spent significant time with them. They found it very difficult to see their grandchildren less often. It left a gaping hole in their lives.

Does this sound familiar to you? It's a natural part of life and growing up, but something challenging for a grandparent to come to terms with.

I raise this because it's a transition you will have to make at some point, if you have grandchildren now or in the future. What does this mean for how you approach grandparenting?

Naturally, you will want to spend many special hours with your grandchildren. However, you should also ensure that this doesn't come at the expense of neglecting your friendships and activities. Recognising that this transition will probably happen eventually helps you prepare emotionally. It also allows you to accept that your relationship will change, and you will need to adjust.

How Do You Form New Friendships as You Age and After Retirement?

This is an evergreen topic when coaching clients about their retirement planning.

Forming friendships later in life requires more intentional effort than when you're younger, but it's possible and often leads to deeper, more meaningful connections.

Start with shared interests and activities. Join clubs, classes, or groups centred around things you genuinely enjoy (book clubs, hiking groups, volunteer organisations, hobby clubs, or fitness classes). Shared or team activities help facilitate natural conversation and regular opportunities to see the same people, which is crucial for building familiarity and trust.

For example, if you are an outdoor enthusiast who enjoys walking, joining a walking club. You could also venture out on hiking trails in Australia, which is an easy way to meet new people. I recently walked the Three Capes Trail in Tasmania and met so many different people. Some genuine friendships were formed, and we are still in contact. What struck me was that people who love nature and hiking tend to share common values, which, in and of itself, makes it easier to strike up a friendship.

A Friendship Building Tip

These practical examples could be the push that gets you started; why not give them a go?

- Three months: Give new activities three months of attendance before discerning the friendship potential.

- Two initiatives: Take the initiative in at least two conversations or invitations per potential friendship.

- One personal share: Share one meaningful personal experience to test relationship depth.

The Friendship Funnel Approach

- Wide net: Start with many casual connections through various activities.
- Regular contact: Maintain consistent interaction with those who seem compatible.
- Deeper engagement: Gradually increase time and intimacy with the most promising connections.
- Quality over quantity: Focus energy on 3-5 potential close friendships rather than trying to be friends with everyone.

Embrace new learning opportunities. Take classes at community colleges, attend workshops, or join discussion groups. Learning environments naturally foster connection as people share the experience of discovering something new together.

The University of the Third Age offers a wide range of courses on diverse topics and interests. If you enjoy learning new things or are simply curious about life, this is an excellent opportunity to meet people. I love their tagline on their website: learn, laugh, live!

Volunteer for causes you care about. This attracts like-minded people and creates bonds through shared purpose. Whether it's helping at a food bank, mentoring young people, or supporting local charities, volunteering often leads to lasting friendships.

This topic is covered in Chapter Seven, Your Work, so there's no need to repeat myself. Adopting a person-centred approach to life and endeavouring to support people in the community profoundly enhances one's sense of well-being and overall health.

Be patient with the process. Adult friendships tend to develop more slowly than those formed in childhood. People have established routines and family obligations and may be more cautious about opening up to you. Don't get discouraged if connections take time to deepen.

Make the first move. Suggest coffee after a class, invite someone to lunch, or propose a walk together. Many people want to connect but are waiting for someone else to initiate.

If you are the person who waits for others to take the initiative, step out of your comfort zone and be the first to invite someone to join you for coffee. You may surprise yourself and realise it's not that hard.

Consider your neighbours and community. Attend local events, join neighbourhood associations, or try to chat with people you see regularly. Geographic proximity can be a foundation for friendship.

Be genuinely interested in others. Ask questions about their experiences, listen actively, and remember details from previous conversations. Show curiosity about their lives and perspectives.

Some people naturally prefer privacy and don't like being asked questions. If you keep your awareness sharp, you'll quickly pick up on a stranger's discomfort. Pay attention to their signs and subtle cues and act accordingly. However, I've noticed that most people, when you show genuine interest, will happily chat openly about themselves. Sometimes, they'll talk your ear off!

Stay open to different types of people. You might find meaningful connections with people who seem different from you initially but share your values or sense of humour.

The key is consistency. Showing up regularly to the same activities or places increases your chances of developing the repeated interactions that friendships need to grow.

Digital Tools to Support Retirement Friendships

While face-to-face interaction remains crucial, technology can enhance your ability to build friendships:

- Meetup apps help find local groups with shared interests.
- Social media helps maintain connections with distant friends.
- Video calls enable regular contact with family and friends.
- Shared digital activities like online games or virtual book clubs.
- Neighbourhood apps connect you with local community members.

The key is to use technology to facilitate actual connections rather than replace them.

Overcoming Retirement Friendship Obstacles

When life throws obstacles at you, it's always better to look for ways to overcome and push through and find a practical solution. Here are some ideas when facing particular challenges:

- Energy and Health Limitations: When this occurs, focus on low-energy social activities when needed, such as coffee dates, phone calls, or home visits, rather than demanding activities.

- Geographic Isolation: If you've moved or live in a regional or remote area, consider online communities, travel groups, and other social opportunities that can provide support.

- Social Anxiety: Start with structured activities in which conversation topics are built in (e.g., community clubs, classes, volunteer work) rather than unstructured social gatherings.

- Past Relationship Hurt: Don't let previous friendship disappointments prevent new connections. Each relationship is unique, and life experiences can often help us become better friends.

As David Bowie discovered after experiencing global fame, the relationships we build with family and close friends ultimately matter most. In retirement, you have the precious gift of time to invest in these connections, nurturing existing relationships and building new ones.

Your friendships and family networks in retirement become sources of joy and support. They also greatly strengthen the foundations of physical health, mental well-being, and overall life satisfaction. The effort you put into building and maintaining these friendships and relationships might be the most important work you do in retirement, providing benefits that grow over time.

Remember that meaningful relationships require vulnerability, consistency, and mutual investment. The rewards, the laughter shared, the burdens lightened, the celebrations enhanced, and the simple comfort of knowing you matter to others make this effort worthwhile.

Reflection Questions for a Thriving Retirement

1. How many close friends do you have? How often do you see them? When last did you see them?

2. When was the last time you went away with your family, and when was the last time you had an uninterrupted family meal together (sans mobile phones within reach!)?

3. How and where were your current friendships formed? How many are close friends, acquaintances of convenience, activity friends, etc.?

4. When was the last time you formed a new friendship?

5. Would you like to initiate new friendships? If so, what are you prepared to do to make this happen?

6. What role does your family play in your life?

7. What do your close friends mean to you?

8. Which relationships in your life feel most authentic, and what makes them special?

9. Are there friendships that have become one-sided? How might you address this?

10. What friends do you turn to for different needs (emotional support, fun and laughter, advice, or pursuing shared interests)?

11. How well do your current friends know the 'real you' versus just your social persona?

12. How do you prefer to stay connected with friends (face to face, phone calls, texting, social media)?

13. Are you better at maintaining friendships or initiating contact, and how could you improve in the area where you are challenged?

14. What prevents you from reaching out to friends more often, and how could you overcome these barriers?

15. How comfortable are you with being vulnerable and sharing more profound thoughts or struggles with friends?

16. How have your friendships changed as you've traversed different life stages, and what patterns do you notice?

17. Which friendships have survived significant life changes, and what made them resilient?

18. How might retirement affect your current friendships, especially work-related ones?

19. What friendships would you like to reconnect with, and what's stopping you?

20. How has your relationship with family members evolved, and where would you like to see growth?

21. What family traditions or regular gatherings are important to you, and how can you nurture these?

22. If you have children, how do you balance being supportive without being intrusive?

23. If you have grandchildren, what role do you want to play in your grandchildren's lives, and how will you cultivate those relationships?

24. What activities, interests, or values could serve as a foundation for new friendships?

25. How comfortable are you with putting yourself in social situations where you might meet new people?

26. What fears or hesitations do you have about forming new friendships, and how can you address them?

27. Are you interested in intergenerational friendships, or do you prefer connecting with peers in similar life stages?

28. How do you show appreciation and care for the important people in your life?

29. Are you as good a friend to others as they are to you, and where could you improve?

30. How much time are you willing to invest in maintaining and building relationships?

31. How do you balance your need for social connection with your need for solitude?

32. What boundaries do you need to set in relationships to maintain your well-being?

33. How do you handle conflicts or disagreements with close friends and family members?

34. As you age, what support do you hope to receive from friends and family, and what are you prepared to give?

35. How will you maintain friendships if mobility, health, or technology barriers arise?

36. Beyond close friends and family, what broader social networks or communities provide you with connection and belonging?

37. How important is it to have friends in your local area versus maintaining long-distance relationships?

38. What role do neighbours, acquaintances, and casual social connections play in your overall well-being?

CHAPTER TEN

YOUR LEGACY

'We all die. The goal is not to live forever; the goal is to create something that will.'

—Chuck Palahniuk

'Our days are numbered. One of the primary goals in our lives should be to prepare for our last day. The legacy we leave is not just in our possessions but in the quality of our lives. What preparations should we be making now? The greatest waste in all of our earth, which cannot be recycled or reclaimed, is our waste of the time that God has given us each day.'

—Bill Graham

'If you would not be forgotten as soon as you are dead, either write something worth reading or do something worth writing.'

—Benjamin Franklin

What is a legacy? Depending on who you ask, you will undoubtedly receive a variety of definitions.

In many respects, it's the answer to two questions: For what do you want to be remembered? What do you want to leave behind for your loved ones to support them in life (often in monetary form), as a reminder of you and your love for them?

As you can imagine, when people answer these questions, you most certainly end up with a wide range of ways to leave a legacy.

Legacy is ultimately about influence, the ripple effects of a person's life that continue long after they are gone. In this sense, everyone leaves a legacy, whether intentional or not. The question is whether you want to be deliberate about shaping that influence.

Adopting a broader approach to one's legacy is preferable. Leaving money is meaningful, but it is only one of a plethora of different ways to leave a legacy.

It comes down to the who, what, and how of the nature of the legacy that is most important to you. For some people, it's all about the impact on society, science, and a community. For other people, it's the preservation of something they may have invented, initiated, or implemented. Passing on something meaningful and possibly helpful to immediate and extended family, as well as close friends, is more important to others.

For someone else, giving back to society through a specific contribution can be a satisfying and fulfilling accomplishment.

A concept to consider: the legacy you leave may be open to interpretation and may mainly depend on the perception of others, i.e. people known to you and people to whom you may bequeath your legacy. So, the way your legacy is received is typically not within your control; however, it is certainly something you can influence.

Focusing on your legacy may provide a higher purpose. What do I mean by that? If you are approaching retirement, it may be challenging to determine your purpose for the next twenty to thirty years;

it may take some time to clarify. You may find it easier to reflect on the legacy you wish to leave for your community and/or society. This approach can act as a catalyst for discovering your purpose in retirement.

Identifying Your Legacy and The Challenge It Creates

Remembering that legacy is something handed down or passed on; it can be a very confronting topic for people who have a fear of dying. This can also apply to individuals who have a zest for life and a passion for living and who are in denial about their own mortality.

The reasons for finding the topic of legacy confronting are complex, some of which include:

- Confronting Mortality: Thinking about legacy compels individuals to acknowledge their finite existence. For many, this is the first time they've seriously contemplated death as a reality rather than an abstract concept. This realisation of mortality can trigger anxiety, sadness, or existential dread that feels overwhelming. Consequently, for some people, avoidance becomes a coping mechanism.

- Fear of Inadequacy: Retirees might worry whether they have accomplished enough to warrant leaving a meaningful legacy. They may compare themselves to famous figures or successful peers and conclude their lives have not been substantial enough to matter. This can lead to shame about perceived failures or missed opportunities.

- Judgment About Life Choices: The process of creating a legacy involves honest self-reflection on the decisions made throughout one's life. People may need to face regrets about career paths, relationships, or values they compromised. They might fear that examining their life closely will reveal too many disappointments or failures.

- Overwhelming Responsibility: The weight of 'getting it right' can feel paralysing. People worry about choosing the wrong charitable cause, saying the wrong thing in a memoir, or making financial decisions that could harm rather than help their beneficiaries.

I think we have all heard about the reading of wills and how they can tear siblings apart.

- Vulnerability and Exposure: Legacy work often involves sharing personal stories, admitting mistakes, or expressing emotions that feel too private. The fear of being judged by family members or having one's authentic self rejected can be intense.

Overcoming These Concerns and Fears

Start Small and Private: Begin with less intense activities, such as writing in a personal journal, creating a simple photo album, or having casual conversations with family members. This builds confidence without the pressure of making something 'important.'

Reframe the Definition of Legacy: Reflect on the point that legacy isn't meant to be about fame or grand gestures. A legacy can be as simple as teaching a grandchild to bake, sharing work skills with a younger colleague, or consistently showing kindness to neighbours. Every life has value worth preserving.

Focus on Connection, Not Perfection: Emphasise that the goal is about sharing authentic experiences that connect with others. Family members want to understand their loved one's journey, including struggles and mistakes. This makes the person more relatable and human, while also conveying valuable lessons to younger generations.

Use Guided Frameworks: Utilise structured approaches, such as prompted journals, ethical will templates, or organised storytelling formats. Having a framework reduces the sense of uncertainty about where to begin and provides direction for the process.

Accept Imperfection: Leaving a meaningful legacy does not require a person to live a perfect life. Often, the most powerful legacies emerge from sharing experiences of overcoming difficulties, learning from mistakes, or finding fulfilment despite challenges.

Seek Support: Working with a counsellor, joining a group to write a memoir, or partnering with a family member can provide emotional support and practical guidance. Having someone to help process fears and celebrate progress makes the journey less intimidating. Working with a family member may serve to strengthen the familial relationship.

Remember Who Your Recipients Are: Consider the gift and who you intend to give it to. Children want to know their parents' stories, charities need support, and communities benefit from accumulated wisdom. This outward focus helps overcome doubts or internal fears.

The critical point is to recognise that confronting mortality and life's imperfections is part of a legacy's value. It demonstrates courage, authenticity, and the universal human experience of navigating life's complexities.

It is because of the points outlined above that, when supporting my clients on the topic of legacy, I begin by asking them about death and dying before discussing the legacy they wish to leave. Most people avoid talking about and confronting death. It can be an uncomfortable subject, and many people cope with their discomfort through denial or flippancy. So, if I can help a client come to terms with their mortality and find peace with it, that creates a foundation for discussing their legacy.

Once the client is ready to explore what their legacy may look like, I ask them about the areas, issues, and people they feel most deeply about. We also explore the activities, work, and leisure pursuits that have brought them the most satisfaction in their lives. We then discuss the various options available to them. They will narrow the long list down to one or a few options and then research those areas before making any commitment.

This funnelling process ensures their final decision reflects their core values, natural abilities, and genuine sense of self.

Benefits of Working on Your Legacy

Working on a legacy before death can provide profound benefits for retirees that extend far beyond the eventual recipients:

- Sense of Purpose and Meaning: Creating a legacy can provide retirees with a compelling reason to get up each morning. Whether writing a memoir, establishing a scholarship fund, or teaching grandchildren skills, legacy work provides direction and significance.

- Enhanced Mental and Emotional Well-being: Legacy projects often involve reflection, creativity, and connection with others, all of which support cognitive health and emotional resilience. The process of organising life stories, values, and wisdom can have a profoundly positive impact on oneself.

- Strengthened Family Bonds: Collaborating with family members on legacy projects fosters meaningful conversations across generations. Grandparents sharing stories, teaching skills, or involving children in charitable decisions help build stronger relationships and ensure that family history is preserved.

- Active Engagement Versus Passive Waiting: Instead of just hoping their impact will be remembered, retirees can take steps to influence how they will be remembered. This sense of agency and control over their story can be empowering and help lessen any potential anxiety.

- Living to See the Impact: Unlike posthumous bequests, many legacy activities allow retirees to witness the positive effects of their efforts. They can see scholarship recipients succeed, watch family members cherish shared stories, or observe how their mentorship influences others. Releasing funds from the 'bank of mum and dad' to support adult children in securing their own home can bring immense satisfaction.

- Intellectual Stimulation: Legacy work often involves learning new skills, organising complex information, or solving problems related to charitable giving or family planning. This mental engagement can help maintain cognitive function and provide intellectual satisfaction.

- Values Transmission: The process facilitates retirees to articulate what matters most to them and find effective ways to convey those values. This ensures their core beliefs and principles continue to impact future generations.

The act of creating a legacy transforms abstract hope about being remembered into concrete, meaningful action that benefits both the retiree and their intended recipients.

So, the big question is: what do you want to pass on to others? What do you want to leave behind as a gift? How would you like to be remembered? What will people say you stood for?

What will be your legacy? There are many and varied types of legacies that you could leave, but what will be uniquely yours?

Here are different areas and aspects to consider:

Cultural Approaches to Legacy Across the World

Different cultures view legacy through unique lenses that can inspire broader thinking:

- Indigenous Traditions: Many Indigenous cultures emphasise seven-generation thinking, that is, considering how decisions will affect descendants seven generations into the future. This perspective transforms legacy from personal remembrance to intergenerational impact.

- Asian Ancestor Veneration: In many Asian cultures, maintaining family honour and continuing ancestral wisdom is central to legacy. This includes preserving family stories, recipes, traditions, and values through formal and informal practices.

- Scandinavian Life Books: In Norway and Sweden, creating *'livsbøker'* (life books) is a common practice. This involves compiling comprehensive albums that combine photographs, documents, and stories to preserve family history for future generations.

- African Ubuntu Philosophy: The concept of 'I am because we are' emphasises collective legacy, how individual actions contribute to community well-being, and wisdom that transcends personal mortality.

- Mediterranean Family Archives: In Italy and Greece, families often keep detailed records, recipes, and traditions passed down through generations, viewing each family member as a guardian of their shared heritage.

I have a treasured recipe book that my Mum and Dad filled with personal recipes. It has 'pride of place' in our kitchen, and whenever I open it, it evokes happy memories of my parents. A small but significant legacy!

Consider which cultural approaches resonate with your values and circumstances.

Different Approaches to Building Your Legacy

Through the ages, men and women have left significant marks on their communities, sometimes locally, sometimes regionally, at the state level, or even nationally and occasionally globally.

One only needs to consider figures like Mother Teresa, Martin Luther King Jr., Nelson Mandela, and William Wilberforce, who made a profound impact in the countries where they lived, but also influenced people and societies beyond their own.

There are also those who quietly, intentionally, and humbly serve their local communities through volunteering, either independently or via organisations such as Rotary, Lions, Probus, Surf Living Clubs and many others.

So, how do you think you might serve and contribute to your local community and/or beyond, as you transition to the next stage of life?

Here are some suggestions to stimulate your thinking if you haven't yet considered this aspect of your life:

- Leave a legacy through your body of work.
- Endow a scholarship at your alma mater for future students.
- Write a book on a topic you are most passionate about.
- Pass on skills and know-how to organisations, groups, and individuals.

You may have a passion for building organisational capacity or for supporting non-profit organisations working in areas close to your heart. You may have grown up in a particular community and benefited from its many aspects, a place you want to give back to and invest in.

Here are a few areas where you could contribute and have a positive impact:

- Leave money to charities you care about.
- Be a mentor to people who are motivated to learn and grow.
- Volunteer with organisations that support causes you care about.

Legacy Without Traditional Family Structures

Not everyone has children or traditional family structures, but everyone can create a meaningful legacy:

- Chosen Family: Close friends, godchildren, nieces and nephews, or mentees can be recipients of your legacy.
- Institutional Legacy: Establish scholarships, endowments, or programs at organisations meaningful to you.
- Community Impact: Volunteering, community projects, or advocacy can create lasting, positive change.
- Creative or Intellectual Legacy: Books, art, inventions, or innovations that contribute to human knowledge or culture.
- Environmental Legacy: Conservation efforts, sustainable practices, or environmental restoration that benefit future generations.

Professional Legacy: Sharing Your Wisdom

Your decades of professional experience represent valuable knowledge that can benefit others:

- Mentoring Programs: Many organisations have formal or informal mentoring programs that enable retirees to share their expertise with younger professionals.
- Industry Documentation: Consider writing about changes you have witnessed in your field, innovations you were part of, or lessons learned from career challenges.

- Skills Transfer: Conduct workshops, develop training materials, or volunteer to share technical expertise with community organisations, schools, or non-profits.

- Professional Archives: Donate significant work documents, photographs, or artifacts to industry museums, professional organisations, or relevant historical societies.

- Beyond Money: Consider passing on financial wisdom, values about money, and lessons about generosity and responsibility.

- Charitable Giving Strategy: If philanthropy is important to you, consider involving family members in decisions about charitable giving to teach valuable lessons and create a shared purpose. We encouraged our children to pledge to not-for-profit organisations from an early age.

- Family Financial Education: Share your experience with investments, business ownership, or financial mistakes as learning opportunities for younger family members.

Your Memoir

Do you enjoy writing? My father-in-law and my father both penned their memoirs before they passed away. Regarding my father-in-law, he created three leather-bound copies and handed them to his daughters about fifteen years before his death.

In my father's case, his memoirs were a work in progress until his death. In both cases, they were very special gifts to their children and grandchildren. They provide precious insights into their respective characters, illuminating aspects that were not necessarily obvious or even known during their lifetimes.

These documents are the legacy that will stand the test of time and pass through future generations. A memoir is a priceless gift, providing insights into earlier generations to current and future generations.

Writing a memoir can be very satisfying and rewarding, as it involves looking back on one's life with thankfulness and gratitude, and reflecting on the years ahead with anticipation and optimism.

Recipients of a memoir might find it a source of joy and comfort. Offspring may especially value having a tangible record of a family member's life, beyond photos in a frame.

Questions to ponder before you commence writing your memoir:

What would you like to have known about your parents that was not self-evident or disclosed during their lifetime?

Reflecting on this question may provide you with valuable insights into what your children would like to know about you. There may also be areas they are aware of, but you could elaborate on them further.

What would you like to have known about yourself from the perspective, knowledge, and observations of your parents?

Once again, this will help you think about what you could write about your children (i.e., sharing some of the joys, heartaches, and special memories you have of them).

So, how would you like to leave behind meaningful memories for your children?

Perhaps ask them what they'd like to know about you that they don't already know, or what they'd like to learn about themselves from your perspective.

Just imagine the rich conversations that could unfold and the self-discovery that could result.

Some Helpful Tips and Formats for Writing Your Memoir

Often, the most challenging part of writing is getting started and having a framework to work within. As Lao Tzu once said, '*The journey of a thousand miles begins with a single step.*'

Some planning tips to get you underway:

- Curate Materials: Photos, letters, documents, journals.
- Set a Schedule: Dedicate specific times for writing.
- Choose Your Medium: Handwritten, typed, video or voice recorded.

- Decide on Length: Short vignettes or longer chapters.
- Consider Your Audience: Who will be reading your memoir?

Writing Prompts

To stimulate your thinking and idea generation, here are some areas to consider writing about and questions to answer:

Your family:

- What they mean to you.

- Why have they been special in your life?

- Happy memories of family holidays, gatherings, and dinner conversations.

- What you appreciate about them and the gifts you see in them.

- Your recollections of their character and their passions.

- Your hopes for their future.

- Your love for them.

Your life:

- What is the first memory you can recall?

- Describe a typical day in your childhood home.

- What was your biggest fear as a child?

- Think about and describe a time you felt incredibly proud.

- What is the best advice you have ever received?

- Describe a moment when you felt truly alive.

- Describe a moment when you felt deeply fulfilled and contented.

- What's something you wish you had done differently?

- Who has had the most significant influence on your life?

- What do you hope people will remember about you?

Begin where you feel most comfortable. Writing chronologically will be helpful for some but an obstacle for others, so work with what suits your personality best. It is not a bad idea to include ordinary moments, as daily life details and memories are often the most treasured. Be honest, as your family will, in most cases, respect authenticity and find it more valuable than perfection.

One area that many children and spouses may appreciate is learning about parts of your life you didn't share during your lifetime. You may not have shared these because you thought no one would be interested. You may have avoided sharing these areas because you thought your family or close friends might find them insensitive or potentially hurtful. That's where the many years of living and the associated wisdom and discernment you've gained will come into play.

I remember sharing something very personal from my teenage years with my children while we were on holiday. They said how much they appreciated hearing about that part of my life. It seemed to me at the time that showing vulnerability meant a lot to them.

My dad was the epitome of a gentleman and a very private and humble person. He was also a man of few words; some would say a solitary man, a quality that was particularly evident in group settings. However, whenever he was in an environment conducive to recounting his escapades in the Second World War, it was a challenge to stop him!

Following his passing, my brother Alan and I had to sort through his belongings and the copious letters and documents that he had stored away in a black box in the attic. This box intrigued us as kids. What was inside? Were there deep secrets from the past? Or perhaps a priceless artifact? When we opened this treasure chest of a black box, we discovered a side of my father that had remained a mystery while he was alive.

Through various documents and certificates, we discovered that he had been the head boy of his school and had achieved the highest academic position in his final year. He also ranked fourth in the entire British Commonwealth in 'The College of Preceptors' examination. It was heartening to learn about our father's achievements, but at the same time, it left us wondering why he had not mentioned them to us while he was alive.

When reflecting on the stories, memories, and history you believe are essential to leave as a legacy for your children, grandchildren, and siblings, think about the aspects they will want to remember about you when you're gone. This is especially important for your children. Never assume that some parts of your life may hold little or no significance to your family.

If your parents have passed, you will recall those moments when you may have felt that a part of you, your life, and your family were irrevocably lost. Perhaps during these times of reflection, you wish you had a virtual vault to visit and hear what your parents were thinking or feeling at different stages of their lives. You may love to understand what they wished for you in your childhood and beyond, and what memories they cherish from your early years.

Having these moments in a 'time capsule' might help keep you connected to your family's lives after you leave this mortal coil!

 Write as if you're speaking to your beloved family members. Grammar need not be perfect. What truly matters are the insights into your life and character, and that's what will be most valued. Sharing your emotions will also be appreciated; each of us has an emotional side, so it's perfectly normal to share the highs and lows of life with perspective.

There are many different formats you could choose:

- Themes related to your life, such as work and family.

- In a letter format, i.e., 'to my children', etc.

- A 'life's lessons approach', i.e., what you learned during your life in different contexts and therefore what counsel and wisdom you wish to pass on to the reader.

An alternative is to structure your memoir according to the seasons of your life, i.e.:

- Early Years (0-18): Childhood, family dynamics, formative experiences.

- Learning & Growing (18-25): Education, first jobs, early relationships.

- Building Life (25-40): Career development, marriage, starting a family.
- Peak Years (40-65): Achieving career goals, raising children, and participating in sports and cultural activities.
- Transition (65+): Retirement, grandchildren, reflection and community involvement.

Some questions you could answer in each season:

- What were the defining moments of this season?
- Who were the most important people in your life at that time?
- What challenges did you face, and how did you overcome them?
- What values or beliefs shaped your decisions?
- What would you tell your younger self about this time?

Helpful Tools to Tell Your Story

If you're interested in exploring your memoir or a similar project, here is a selection of tools to assist you in recording your legacy:

- Video Interviews:

  StoryCorps is an American company that only supports people throughout the USA; however, their concept may inspire you to conduct your own interviews and record your story for your children and posterity.

  https://storycorps.org/

  StoryWorth allows users to record their responses to a series of prompts about themselves and their lives. Alternatively, it will support you in asking questions of a relative over time. Once the questions have been answered, a book will be published as a gift for children, grandchildren, and close friends. The book also accommodates the insertion of photos and other anecdotes.

  StoryWorth (https://welcome.storyworth.com/)

  A good friend recently undertook a project using StoryWorth to record the life and times of her ageing parents. She thoroughly enjoyed interviewing her parents and shared many laughs in response to their differing recollections of their life experiences. Once completed, she presented a bound copy to her parents, siblings, and children. Memories for generations, captured in an album of words and pictures!

There are a few apps that will achieve similar outcomes to Story Corps and StoryWorth:

- Memlife. This free app enables you to record your story and then convert it into a book that includes both text and images.

  https://memlife.com/home

- LegacyStories. This offers a free plan with limited storage capacity. If you require unlimited storage capacity for all your video recordings, photos, and text, a commercial plan is available, but it is quite expensive.

  https://legacystories.org/

Your Digital Legacy

It's prudent for retirees to consider their digital footprint and electronic legacy in the following ways:

- Digital Asset Management:

  Organise and provide access instructions for photo libraries, email accounts, social media profiles, and digital documents. Consider creating a comprehensive digital inventory for your executor.

- Online Storytelling Platforms:

  Beyond the tools already mentioned, consider modern platforms like:

  FamilySearch: Create digital family trees with stories and photos.

  Legacy.com: Maintain ongoing memorial pages that families can contribute to and update.

- Google's Inactive Account Manager:

  Ensure critical digital assets are transferred appropriately.

- Social media memorialization**:**

  Most platforms offer options for maintaining profiles as memorial spaces.

- Digital Ethical Wills:

  Record video messages for specific life events your family will experience (graduations, weddings, births of great-grandchildren). These time-capsule messages can be profound.

- Virtual Reality Preservation:

  Some families are experimenting with 360-degree video recordings of family gatherings, homes, and storytelling sessions, creating an immersive experience for future generations.

Legacy Maintenance and Evolution

Legacy creation is more than a one-time project. As you age and circumstances change, your legacy may evolve. A memoir might become a series of shorter stories. A charitable foundation might transition to volunteer work. Stay flexible and allow your legacy to grow and change as you do.

Your achievements or the size of your investment portfolio does not define your legacy. Instead, it is shaped by the love, wisdom, kindness, and positive impact you share with others. Every chat with a grandchild, every act of service, every story told, and every value demonstrated adds to the legacy you leave behind.

The beauty of working on your legacy is that you are actively shaping how your life's influence will continue. In doing so, you may discover that creating your legacy is one of your most fulfilling and purposeful endeavours in your retirement.

As Maya Angelou said, 'People will forget what you said, people will forget what you did, but people will never forget how you made them feel.' That feeling, conveyed through your stories, values, and enduring influence, becomes your legacy.

Reflection Questions for a Thriving Retirement

1. Have you ever considered what you would like your legacy to be?

2. How would you like to be remembered, and in what way?

3. Have you asked your loved ones what they would still like to know about you?

4. What principles have guided your life that you want to pass on to future generations?

5. What positive impact have you made in other people's lives? How can you expand this?

6. What problems in the world do you feel passionate about contributing solutions to?

7. How do you want your life's work to be remembered and built upon?

8. What family stories, traditions, or wisdom do you want to ensure get passed down?

9. What life lessons would be valuable for your children and or grandchildren?

10. How do you want to be remembered as a parent, grandparent, sibling, or friend?

11. What personal qualities do you hope others will remember about you?

12. Are you interested in creating something lasting (writing, art, music, crafts, or projects) that will outlive you?

13. What items, collections, or possessions have special meaning that you'd like to pass on?

14. Would you like to document your story through some form of memoir?

15. What spaces or places have been important to you that you'd like to help preserve?

16. What expertise, skills, or knowledge do you possess that could benefit others if shared?

17. Who in your life could benefit from your guidance, and how will you offer this?

18. What institutions or causes would you like to support?

19. How can you contribute to the education or development of future generations?

20. What charities that align with your values would benefit from your support?

21. Are you interested in creating ongoing giving through foundations, scholarships, etc.?

22. How can you teach financial wisdom and responsibility to the next generation?

23. What unfinished relationship business do you want to address (apologies to make, gratitude to express, or reconciliations to pursue)?

24. How do you want to heal or transform any negative family dynamics?

25. What love, encouragement, or support do people in your life still need from you?

26. How can you strengthen the relationships between others in your family or community?

27. How can you contribute to the health and vitality of your local community?

28. What environmental stewardship do you want to model and promote?

29. Which aspects of your legacy do you want to work on immediately versus later in life?

30. What conversations do you need to have with family about your legacy wishes?

31. What legal or practical steps do you need to take to fulfil your legacy intentions?

32. How will you measure whether you're successfully building the legacy you desire?

33. How do you want to continue evolving so that your legacy best reflects you?

34. What would you regret not doing or saying if you knew your time was limited?

35. How can you live each day in a way that builds the legacy you want to leave?

36. Who will carry forward the values and work that matter most to you after you're gone?

37. How can you inspire others to build on the positive changes you've initiated?

38. What systems can you put in place to ensure your legacy has a lasting impact?

CHAPTER ELEVEN

YOUR FINAL DAYS

'When you are sorrowful, look again in your heart, and you shall see that in truth you are weeping for that which has been your delight.'

—Kahlil Gibran

'Dying is nothing to fear. It can be the most wonderful experience of your life. It all depends on how you've lived.'

—Dr Elisabeth Kubler-Ross

Across cultures worldwide, death is approached in different ways. From the Mexican Día de los Muertos celebration of departed loved ones, to the Tibetan understanding of death as a transition, to the Japanese concept of *ikigai* (life's purpose), which includes preparing for a meaningful end. Yet universally, preparation brings peace.

A person may die gradually from a terminal illness, suddenly in a tragic accident, or pass away naturally due to old age.

Death is final and absolute. There's no second chance to wake up and do the things you have always wanted to do or say the things you always meant to say to loved ones. There's no coming back!

We all know that in life, there are two certainties: death and taxes. Those who pay taxes do so either begrudgingly or willingly. So, what about death? Facing the reality of death and coming to terms with it (albeit this may take time) will help ensure that our days count and lead to a flourishing life in retirement.

Many people are fearful of dying and will do everything possible to preserve their lives, sometimes at the expense of positively experiencing life and living well! Some people who fall into this dynamic are sometimes labelled 'worry warts' because they worry about everything. This is naturally an unhealthy way to live. It robs you of joy, happiness, contentment, and inner peace.

The Bible is full of wise advice for living. On the topic of worrying, Luke 12:25-26 states: *'Who of you, by worrying, can add a single hour to his life? Since you cannot do this very little thing, why do you worry about the rest?'* Sage advice, but the reality can naturally be very challenging.

As will be explained in detail below, the key antidote to worrying about death is preparing for it.

Reaching Acceptance of Death and Dying

When we come to terms with our mortality, accepting that our time here is limited, as is that of every other living being, something remarkable can occur. We can feel a deep serenity and, in turn, open ourselves to experiencing life more fully. Naturally, this is a process that requires time and effort.

Kübler-Ross's book 'On Death and Dying' discusses five stages of grief related to death and dying: denial, anger, bargaining, depression, and acceptance.

Kubler Ross' Change Management Model

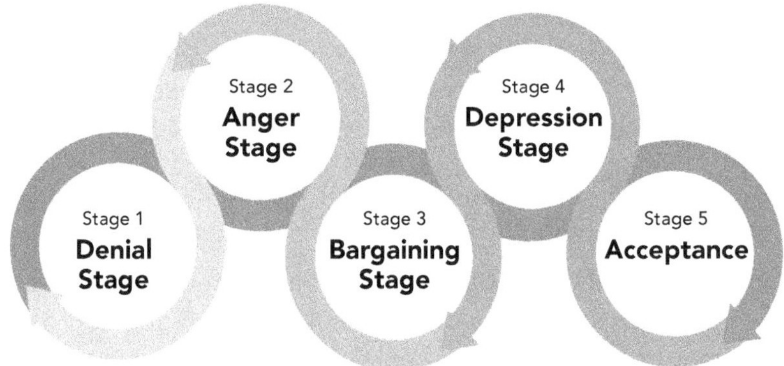

Source: Kübler-Ross, Five Stages of Grief Model

Concerning accepting death as a reality, people typically react in different ways; we might:

- Viscerally experience all five stages over a prolonged period.
- Experience all five stages and oscillate between them before reaching acceptance.
- Spend very little time in all stages before transitioning to acceptance.
- Oscillate between each stage on multiple occasions before reaching acceptance.
- Never find peace and acceptance.

People experience grief and the journey to acceptance in different ways. The model isn't meant to be linear, and most of the time, it doesn't mean progressing sequentially through each stage until reaching acceptance. The way people arrive at acceptance and how they navigate that journey is important. For some, it will be a short process; for others, it may take much longer.

Consider creating your own timeline for reaching acceptance. Avoid rushing the process. Track your emotional journey. It may be helpful to regularly journal about your feelings about mortality, noting shifts in your perspective over time.

A helpful way to gain acceptance about death and dying is to talk about it with close friends and family, and a counsellor, if needed.

You may very well be thinking to yourself now: *'Well, that's easier said than done. So practically speaking, how will I reach acceptance when it's so confronting to think about it at a deep level?'*

Reflect on and attempt to live out some of these suggestions, being open to how they might assist you:

- Normalise death by recognising that it is a natural part of the life cycle. Be curious about how different cultures approach death (you may be encouraged by what you uncover). Volunteering at a hospice for several months can assist with acceptance by observing how people have reached that stage.

- Review your life so far, reflecting on your accomplishments, contributions, and the impact you have made in all aspects of your life. Think of all the healthy relationships you've experienced so far. Acknowledge the mistakes you've made along life's journey without beating yourself up. Importantly, celebrate the richness and uniqueness of your life.

- Spend time thinking about the meaning of your life. Recognise how your life has mattered over the years, and the positive influence you've had on friends, colleagues, and strangers. What about your relationship with your siblings, your own family, and your life partner? Acknowledge the love and care you have given and be thankful for the love you have received at different times in your life.

Spiritual Preparation

Earlier in the book, I mentioned the flywheel of life and its various components, one of which is your spiritual dimension. Take the time to explore your beliefs about the afterlife and what happens to you when you die.

Be open and curious by engaging with faith-based communities. You may find practices such as prayer, meditation, and mindfulness helpful in attaining the peace you desire.

Spiritual preparation looks different for each person. For some, it means deepening their connection to traditional faiths, such as Christianity, Judaism, Islam, Hinduism, Buddhism, or other belief systems. For others, it means exploring secular philosophies about life's purpose and legacy. Some find solace in nature.

It is helpful to recognise that we all have an innate yearning for spiritual meaning in our lives. So, take a balanced approach by being open to exploring what gives your life meaning and how that extends beyond your physical presence.

Finally, think about how you can let go by releasing the need to control outcomes. Be willing to accept help and support from friends, family and professionals. Be open to letting go of making long-term plans. Instead, focus on today and tomorrow rather than five to ten years. This approach can help you live and thrive in the present rather than dwell on the future.

Try these daily practices to help gain perspective:

- Express gratitude for each day.
- Maintain hope while accepting reality.
- Find beauty in small moments, such as watching a bee pollinate a flower.
- Cherish the connections you have with people in your life.
- Focus on making the most of the time left.

Case Study: Gaining a sense of what people do to prepare themselves and their families for a death in the family.

Maria, 68, from Melbourne, discovered that discussing death openly was a transformative experience. Coming from a Hispanic background where death was more accepted as part of life, she organised 'life review' dinners with her adult children. Each month, they would share family stories, discuss values, and talk about hopes for the future. These conversations reduced fear and brought the family closer together. When Maria's mother passed peacefully two years later, the family felt prepared and united.

How to Carefully and Intentionally Prepare for Your Death

When preparing for our death, there are many aspects to consider, including practical matters and personal preparations. It is highly personal, and each person's approach to preparation may vary.

I think it's safe to say that it would be unrealistic to think we can eliminate all fear or sadness about dying. However, by being pragmatic, we can reduce unnecessary anxiety through preparation and finding peace with the natural cycle of life. People find that facing mortality deepens their appreciation for the time they have left. May this be the case for you!

Here is your practical guide, which you can also use as a helpful checklist if that makes it easier for you to navigate this area. As you compile this comprehensive list of areas, it will be wise and advantageous to consult with the following people, where appropriate.

1. Your family

2. Your Financial Advisor

3. Your Accountant

4. Your General Practitioner

Legal and Financial Preparation

Your Will

Many clients I consult with did not have a will when they first engaged me for retirement coaching. It's a common area of neglect. So, make sure you have one, and consider engaging a lawyer to help you. If you need to update your will later in life, you can complete a codicil, which is essentially an amendment to your will and supersedes relevant sections of it as highlighted in the codicil.

Areas to consider when developing or amending your will:

• Specify how your assets are to be distributed (tip: allocation by percentages instead of monetary figures is less complicated, as your circumstances may have changed since writing the will).

- Name an executor and a backup executor (preferably an organisation rather than an individual, albeit this will incur costs).
- Include specific bequests for charities and sentimental items for family and friends.
- Update regularly as circumstances change.
- Keep the original in a secure place and give copies to trusted people.

You can include a provision in your will to allocate money for your children and grandchildren, where appropriate. Consider this: if you have children who are financially secure, would it be more beneficial to invest in a good education for your grandchildren?

Consider provisioning for tangible gifts that you would like to give to special people. My father-in-law was a successful civil engineer by day and a highly talented carpenter on weekends. He handcrafted three magnificent grandfather clocks, one for each of his daughters. The clocks included engraved messages to his daughters. Today, the clocks hang proudly in their respective living rooms, enhancing the rooms' aesthetics and serving as a warm reminder of their father. His legacy lives on in their homes.

Advanced Healthcare Directives

It's worthwhile to plan and implement measures related to your health and related matters. The last thing you want is for your children or close friends to have to make tough decisions without explicit instructions.

Some practical areas to discuss and establish:

- A living will that specifies end-of-life medical preferences.
- Healthcare power of attorney, which designates who the decision-maker is.
- Physician instructions for life-preserving medical treatment, wherever appropriate.
- Organ donation preferences clearly stated, if applicable.

Power of Attorney Documents

- Power of attorney for financial and legal decisions.
- An enduring power of attorney that remains valid if you are incapacitated.
- Choose someone trustworthy and financially responsible.

Financial Organisation

- List bank accounts, investment accounts, share portfolio, and retirement funds.
- Include account numbers, contact information, and instructions on where to find passwords.
- Designate beneficiaries on all accounts.
- Keep the list updated and accessible to the executor.

Insurance Policies

- Life insurance policies with beneficiaries updated.
- Disability insurance information.
- Property insurance details.
- Contact information for all insurance agents.

Debt Management

- List all outstanding debts and payment schedules.
- Consider paying off high-interest debt.
- Ensure someone knows about ongoing obligations.

Tax Preparation

- Organise tax documents for easy access.
- Consider prepaying taxes if the estate is expected to owe money.
- Provide the accountant's contact information.

Practical Daily Life Preparations

Digital Asset Management

Online Accounts

- Create a comprehensive list of all online accounts.
- Include usernames, passwords, and security questions.
- Consider using a password management service.

Identify and note the most suitable person to provide this information to, whether it be the executor, lawyer, or another relevant party.

Digital Legacy Planning

- Decide the fate of social media accounts.
- Organise digital photos and videos.
- Transfer critical digital files to a compatible and accessible format.
- Cancel unnecessary subscriptions.

Home and Property

Property Documentation

- Deeds, mortgage information, and property tax records.
- Home maintenance schedules and service provider contacts.
- Location of essential items (jewellery, documents, keys, passwords, etc.).
- Instructions for ongoing property care.

Personal Belongings

- Create an inventory of valuable items.
- Designate recipients for specific items.
- Donate or dispose of unnecessary possessions.
- Organise essential documents in an accessible location.

Daily Operations

Service Providers

- List all service providers (utilities, gardening services, housekeeping).
- Include contact information and payment schedules.
- Arrange for transition or cancellation.

Recurring Obligations

- Automatic bill payments and subscriptions.
- Ongoing commitments (board positions, volunteer work).
- Pet care arrangements.
- Club membership.

Medical and Healthcare Preparation

Medical Information Organisation

- Current medications and dosages.
- Medical history and ongoing conditions.
- Allergies and adverse reactions.
- Contact information for all healthcare providers.

End-of-Life Care Preferences

- Preferred location for dying (home, hospital, hospice).
- Pain management preferences.
- Comfort measures desired.
- Spiritual needs and preferences.

Family Medical History

- Compile a comprehensive family medical history.
- Include genetic information that might affect descendants.
- Organise in a format accessible to family members.

Emotional and Relational Preparation

Relationship Closure

- Reach out to estranged family members or friends.

- Have difficult conversations that need resolution.

- Express forgiveness where appropriate.

- Seek forgiveness for past mistakes.

Expressing Love and Gratitude

- Tell important people how much they mean to you.

- Write letters to be opened after death.

- Share specific memories and their significance.

- Tell your immediate family and siblings how much you love them and what they mean to you.

- Express pride in children's and grandchildren's accomplishments.

Communication Planning

Family Meetings

- Discuss inheritance plans openly.

- Explain the reasoning behind decisions.

- Address potential conflicts before they arise.

- Ensure everyone understands their responsibilities.

Funeral and Memorial Planning

- Specify burial or cremation preferences.

- Choose a funeral home or cremation service provider.

- Plan the funeral or memorial service details and document them.

- Specify whether the coffin should be present at the service or not.

- Prepay arrangements if desired.

- Communicate preferences to family.

You might feel a bit overwhelmed once you realise how much pre-paratory work is involved. The key point to always keep in mind is that you don't want family members to have to deal with all of this after you've passed and they are grieving.

To motivate yourself to act, consider this idea: once you finish this list of actions, you will experience a great sense of relief and be able to move forward, free from this distraction, and thrive in life.

Here is a very practical, prioritised action plan to follow, which will make the process much less burdensome:

Immediate Priorities

- Create or update your will and healthcare directives.
- Organise financial account information.
- Have an honest conversation with family about wishes.
- Choose a healthcare proxy and a financial power of attorney.

Medium-term (4-8 months, depending on your situation and context)

- Complete digital asset inventory.
- Organise essential documents.
- Begin legacy projects (memoir, letters, recordings).
- Address unresolved relationship issues.

Ongoing Practices

- Conduct regular reviews and updates of all documents.
- Continue your work on acceptance, recognising that it's not a linear process.
- Maintain relationships and create new memories.
- Practice gratitude and stay present in the moment. Count your blessings!

Above all, reflect on these helpful points:

- This is a process that takes time, so acceptance happens gradually.
- Seek support from professionals and loved ones in your immediate circle.
- It is okay to experience complex emotions; fear, sadness, and anger are perfectly normal.
- Focus on what you can control. Preparation empowers you in the process.
- Quality of life matters; don't let preparation overshadow living fully in the present.

Death affects everyone eventually; some pass away prematurely, so it's wise to live life to the fullest and appreciate its limited nature, making the most of each day as if it were your last!

In society, the topic of death is somewhat like the big, fat elephant in the room, banished from living room conversations. If it's raised, people will tend to say things like:

'Stop talking like that; please do not be so morbid; can we please change the subject to something brighter and more positive?'

Sound familiar? However, it is vital to engage with this topic, discuss it openly, and ultimately achieve a state of acceptance and peace.

Freed from any anxiety about dying, you can truly make your days count, enjoying each moment, stopping to smell the roses, catching up with a mate for coffee, and simply being.

Life is for living. Once today is over, you'll never get it back, so make sure you make the most of it, in every way.

Remember, it's always better to live life to the fullest, be other-person-centred, and avoid dwelling on regret.

Reflection Questions for a Thriving Retirement

1. Have you ever had a meaningful conversation with anyone about death and dying?

2. If today were your last day on earth, what emotions would you anticipate experiencing?

3. How do you feel about dying?

4. What preparations have you made for your death (e.g., documented what kind of farewell you would prefer, created or updated your will, told your loved ones what they mean to you, how you love them, and what you wish for them in the future, financially organised your farewell, made a list of all your passwords, etc.)?

5. How can you reach acceptance and peace about your finite time on this earth?

PART III

YOUR ACTION PLAN

Now that you have spent some time reflecting and considering questions in the previous eleven chapters about what's important to you, it's time to get specific and turn your thoughts, ideas and intentions into action.

This section is divided into three parts:

Developing your very own retirement plan, with goals, timelines and action points

Implementing your retirement plan and starting to realise the benefits and positive impact of your intentions within the plan.

Understanding and appreciating the role of a Retirement Coach and how they can assist you as you not only develop your plan but also execute it.

CHAPTER TWELVE

DEVELOPING YOUR RETIREMENT PLAN

'If you fail to plan, you are planning to fail.'

—Benjamin Franklin

This chapter outlines setting up and growing a very particular retirement plan, broken into three stages:

- Immediate-term: This covers the areas you need to have addressed by the time you commence retirement or stop your traditional working life.

- Medium-term: Covering most of your retirement. This stage covers the practical steps needed to achieve a viable, flourishing retirement.

- Long-term: Decisions about updating your will, choosing where to live in your later years, and arranging health support if you or your partner becomes ill are all important. Ideally, you should have made these decisions beforehand. These matters should be addressed proactively rather than reactively, as dealing with them under stress can be difficult; something best avoided.

To help you plan for your retirement, try answering these questions:

- When and how do you want to retire?
- How do you want to spend your time in retirement (365 days a year for approximately 30 years plus)?
- What lifestyle do you want to enjoy? What is most important to you?
- How much money do you need annually to maintain your preferred lifestyle?

When is a good time to start planning for your retirement? I remember when I was consolidating my career in my late twenties and early thirties, my retirement fund held little to no interest. That was something far off in the future, something to think about at some point down the track. According to statistics, only two out of ten Australians ever seek financial advice. Therefore, it is reasonable to infer that the same applies to retirement planning; more likely, only one in ten people plan for retirement.

Generally, it's never too early to start planning for your retirement. If you start in your twenties, you will likely be well-provided for by the time you retire. At this stage of your life, you would be well served to focus on the financial aspects of retirement planning.

If you're in your fifties and haven't started retirement planning, it's certainly time to begin. With the average Australian retiring at age 63.8 (Australian Bureau of Statistics, 2024-25), you probably have approximately 4 to 13 years remaining to prepare. As you age, planning becomes increasingly critical.

Before establishing a plan for the three stages outlined above, consider some important foundational work. This will assist you in the planning stage.

To help you become clear about transforming those thoughts and ideas into tangible outcomes, complete the Life Goals form that follows:

In the book Half Time, Bob Buford suggests that for some people, the first half of their lives is focused on success and achievement. He then states that in the second half, if people choose, they can focus on significance. Thinking about this next life stage, what holistic goals* are most important to you? Identify a practical action in each case.

*Holistic goals: *comprehensive, values-based objectives that integrate all aspects of a person's life. They focus on outcomes and, notably, also on the quality of life, relationships, purpose, and sustainability.*

Research from retirement studies worldwide shows that the happiest retirees excel across all these dimensions, not just financially. As you complete this assessment, aim for balance rather than perfection in any single area.

Life Goals

CATEGORY

FAMILY & FRIENDS

Split family and friends into different categories.

GOAL	ACTION
Family:	
Friends:	

SIGNIFICANT OTHER

It could be a 'life partner' or another relationship.

GOAL	ACTION

CAREER

It could be own business, part-time employment, or volunteering.

GOAL	ACTION

FINANCES

It could be financial well-being or financial security.

GOAL	ACTION

HEALTH

It could be emotional, physical, fitness, spiritual, well-being, etc.

GOAL	ACTION

HOME ENVIRONMENT

It may include the home, unit, land, or smallholdings (e.g., 'sea/tree change').

GOAL	ACTION

FUN & LEISURE

Could include sports, hobbies, interests, passions, travel, etc.

GOAL	ACTION

PERSONAL GROWTH

Giving back, e.g., volunteering.

GOAL	ACTION

Make sure to set aside some quality time in a quiet place to reflect on the goals and actions you have identified.

Over the next few weeks, spend time with your partner and or a close friend to discuss your identified goals and obtain their feedback.

If you have a partner, ask them to participate in this experience as well, so that you can ensure both sets of goals are identified and agreed to.

Spend time reviewing your partner's Life Goals while they review yours. As you examine their goals and thoughts, think about what else they might find beneficial, such as hobbies, interests, pursuits, or work. Take notes on your reflections and insights so your thoughts and ideas can be shared rather than lost. Once finished, have an open and honest discussion with your partner and be receptive to their feedback and observations. Consider feedback a gift; without it, we remain unaware of different perspectives and points of view.

Next, ask your partner to complete the following *Self-Assessment Questionnaire* while you complete it as well. Completing this exercise may prompt you to revisit your life goals.

Once again, have an open discussion about each other's questionnaires and their potential implications for the future.

Self-Assessment Questionnaire

Note: There may be some repetition between these questions and those you have answered earlier. This questionnaire is not only designed to help you identify what is important to you, but also for your significant other.

1. Have you already given much thought to retirement? For instance, have you discussed this with your partner, close friends, or financial advisor?

    ____

    ____

    ____

2. What does the word retirement mean to you? When you think of the prospect of retiring, what emotions do you experience?

    ____

    ____

    ____

3. Have you started to plan for your retirement? If yes, what preparation (thinking and or planning) have you initiated or implemented?

    ____

    ____

    ____

4.   What year do you estimate that you would like to retire?

____

____

____

5.   Have you ever considered the concept of a phased retirement (e.g., if you plan to retire in five years, you could work a nine-day fortnight initially and then transition to a four-day week, then three, and then two)?

____

____

____

6.   Have you considered whether you would like to mentor new and less experienced people in your company/organisation, during your final years of employment?

____

____

____

7.   What are your thoughts regarding casual, part-time or volunteer work following retirement?

____

____

____

8.   Where would you like to live once you retire, i.e., stay where you are, move to a smaller place in the same city, move to a smaller rural or semi-urban area, move interstate, overseas, etc.?

____

____

9. How important are cultural connections to your well-being?
    (Consider language communities, cultural centres or religious
    institutions that provide a sense of belonging and identity).

____

____

____

____

10. How important is it for you to be close to your family in
    retirement?

____

____

____

11. What interests and activities do you want to pursue in
    retirement?

____

____

____

12. Are you interested in pursuing further study and or a new
    hobby or interest?

____

____

____

When people who are contemplating retirement fail to develop a holistic plan and a renewed purpose* for their lives, this can have an adverse impact in specific areas:

- Health & well-being (*even death within the first five years of retirement)
- Decisions
- Relationships
- Financial sustainability

The benefits of developing short-term, medium-term, and long-term executable retirement plans are substantial. Benefits include peace of mind, preparing for a fulfilling and active retirement, and planning for a secure future.

Given the potential negative impacts of poor planning, it presents an opportunity for behaviour change. It's about building a solid foundation that leads to positive, life-changing outcomes over time. This foundation depends on proactive planning rather than being caught unprepared on retirement day.

At this stage of developing and later implementing a retirement plan, it is wise to consider consulting a retirement coach for support (covered in Chapter 14).

In life, we may have many great intentions (to lose weight, commit to more regular exercise, spend less time on screens, spend more time with family, achieve a better work-life balance, maintain regular contact with friends, eat a balanced diet, etc.). However, the greatest challenge is to progress from intention to commitment, or, as some would say, actually taking action! Just as people engage a personal trainer to help get fit, a retirement coach will hold a person accountable for implementing their developed retirement plan.

Let's explore the three stages of retirement planning: Immediate, Medium, and Long-Term Plans. By approaching these plans with purpose and dedication, you'll be better equipped to transition into retirement with confidence and peace of mind.

Always consider who can assist you (former employers, colleagues, friends, or your partner) and what research will help inform your decisions. This helps ensure you make the most beneficial choices.

IMMEDIATE PLAN (duration to complete plan: Approximately 6–12 months)

The immediate plan is designed to help you prepare for your upcoming retirement, whether that occurs at the end of the year or within the next two to three years. Ideally, the plan should be completed no later than 12 months before retirement, as it's your pre-retirement plan.

As you work through and develop this plan, here are some questions to ponder:

- Are you planning overseas holidays that will need to be budgeted for in the coming years?
- Are you likely to need a new car in the near term?
- Are you interested in serving on boards, volunteering for a non-profit organisation, etc.?
- If you can scale back your hours, would you consider employment in an area of interest?
- Are there any additional studies that you would like to embark upon in this next season?
- Are there any hobbies or interests you've wanted to pursue for a while but haven't yet?
- Are there people whose counsel you can seek regarding the timing of your retirement?
- Do you have parents or disabled dependents who are reliant on you for financial support?
- Have you considered researching which financial planner to consult about your future?
- Are there any sports you'd like to start playing?

The Immediate Plan is divided into four themes. Complete the goal for each theme and work through what you need to do (Actions) to accomplish this goal. For each action, document when you will start it and when you aim to complete it. Try to be as specific as possible.

E.g., Theme 1: Decide when to retire/transition

Goal: After consulting a financial advisor, seeking the counsel of my retirement coach, and discussing options with a close friend, I will decide by December 2026 whether to transition or retire, and by when in each scenario.

Actions: Research available financial advisors and retirement coaches, choose one of each, and schedule an appointment.

RETIREMENT PLAN: IMMEDIATE TERM

Theme 1: Decide when to retire or transition
GOAL:

ACTIONS	START	COMPLETE

Theme 2: Decisions concerning phased retirement and mentoring
GOAL:

ACTIONS	START	COMPLETE

Theme 3: Developing a financial plan and a will
GOAL:

ACTIONS	START	COMPLETE

Theme 4: Developing a well-being portfolio (Incl. Interests & hobbies in retirement)
GOAL:

ACTIONS	START	COMPLETE

MEDIUM-TERM PLAN (duration to complete the plan: Approximately 6–12 months)

Deciding where to live should not be rushed. There are many factors to consider. Some people prefer to find a retirement living community that offers independent living and the option to transition to long-term care facilities later in life. Others choose to continue living in their existing homes, while some opt to downsize to a smaller house or unit.

Before choosing that coastal property, decide what matters most to you. Is proximity to children, grandchildren, and close friends vital to you? Given that people have a fundamental need for connection, a beautiful house in a quiet location may leave you feeling lonelier than you expect.

Deciding where to live, whether initially or in the medium term, can be a complex topic for discussion. This is well illustrated by a client couple whom I supported:

David wanted to move to a regional mountain town, while Sarah preferred staying near their grandchildren in the city. Their compromise was to keep a small city apartment and buy a mountain cottage, splitting their time 60/40 between the two locations. This solution honoured both their desires and maintained family connections.

Some people may prefer continuing in paid work, albeit in a completely different field from their former career. They would be able to draw on the experience and skills gained during their formal employment years. Transitioning to this next stage of life opens incredible opportunities to become involved in volunteer work and to 'give back' to society, locally and internationally. Many volunteer agencies have staff who can help you find meaningful volunteer assignments.

The guiding principle in these matters is to be open to changing your mind and willing to compromise when it makes sense.

As you work through and develop this plan, here are some questions to ponder:

- Have you factored in stamp duty, transfer fees, and associated costs if you are thinking of purchasing a different home or unit?
- Have you discussed your retirement intentions with your children (particularly where you would like to live)?
- If you plan to downsize from a house to a unit, think about whether you want pets in your new accommodation (always determine whether a unit is pet-friendly).
- Have you worked out whether you need to increase your retirement savings?
- Will you be a self-funded retiree, or will you need to apply for the government pension?

- Have you researched the quality of healthcare services in areas you're considering living?
- If moving internationally, have you investigated healthcare reciprocity agreements?
- Have you thought about how close you are to specialised medical services you might need as you get older?
- How will you stay connected with family and friends using technology?
- What backup systems will you need if technology fails?

When you are ready, try developing your goals and actions for your medium-term plan:

RETIREMENT PLAN: MEDIUM TERM

Theme 1: Decide where to live
GOAL:

ACTIONS	START	COMPLETE

Theme 2: Importance of access to family & friends. Decide what action to take.
GOAL:

ACTIONS	START	COMPLETE

Theme 3: The type of initial accommodation that will be important to me/us.

GOAL:

ACTIONS	START	COMPLETE

Theme 4: Determine whether to sell your current property and whether to purchase a new one.

GOAL:

ACTIONS	START	COMPLETE

Theme 5: Working during retirement (part-time, casual, itinerant, volunteering, etc)

GOAL:

ACTIONS	START	COMPLETE

Theme 6: Financial decisions: investment, divestment, charitable giving, etc
GOAL:

ACTIONS	START	COMPLETE

Theme 7: Technology and Digital Considerations
GOAL:

ACTIONS	START	COMPLETE

Theme 8: Hobbies, Interests and Holiday Considerations
GOAL:

ACTIONS	START	COMPLETE

LONG-TERM PLAN (Approximately 6–12 months)

Decisions about updating your will, where you might live as you approach your twilight years, health support provisions should you and or your partner fall ill, etc.

Please reflect on these areas and discuss them with your partner and or a specialist who can provide expert advice. As you work through and develop this plan, here are some questions to ponder:

- Your will: Have you considered completing end-of-life documents and discussing them with your children?

- Have you considered establishing a power of attorney as a future provision? If so, have you discussed this with the person you have nominated?

- Have you considered the importance, benefits, and value of exercise and the pursuit of diverse interests throughout retirement?

- Have you thought about whether you would ever welcome home care in times of need?

- Have you discussed and agreed with your partner or family whether you expect to eventually transition to a retirement village, nursing home, or assisted living?

- Have you and your partner discussed what end-of-life options you wish to pursue (funeral, memorial service, cremation, donation of your body to medical research, etc.)?

- Have you considered whether to leave a bequest to a charitable organisation?

Theme 1: Decide on later retirement housing/support
GOAL:

ACTIONS	START	COMPLETE

Theme 2: Create a will or review an existing portfolio
GOAL:

ACTIONS	START	COMPLETE

Theme 3: Decisions regarding charitable giving, bequests, and donations
GOAL:

ACTIONS	START	COMPLETE

Theme 4: Decisions regarding health, long-term care, critical illness, funeral expenses, etc.
GOAL:

ACTIONS	START	COMPLETE

As we come to the end of this chapter on developing your retirement plan, I want to introduce you to a couple.

Margaret (63) and James (65) from Toronto were very intentional and completed a comprehensive retirement plan.

However, as they reviewed their plan, they realised that their individual life goals were more aligned than expected, but their timelines differed significantly.

Margaret wanted to retire immediately to care for her ageing mother, while James wanted two more years to complete a significant project.

After much discussion and deliberation, they agreed that Margaret would retire early and assume the caregiving role, while James would continue working. He would, however, negotiate more flexible work arrangements to support Margaret. They would use his continuing income to fund Margaret's early retirement, with a slight adjustment to their monthly budget. This adjustment ensured their savings weren't impacted. This compromise honoured their values and needs.

Planning for any significant life event is important, worthwhile, and beneficial; retirement is no exception. It is essential to put a plan in place that suits you best.

Your retirement plan serves as your initial roadmap, and it can and should evolve as your circumstances change. The value lies in the thoughtful preparation that you invest in it. By working through these exercises, you are already ahead of most people, who often stumble into retirement without a plan.

Reflection Questions for a Thriving Retirement

1. How equipped are you to develop your holistic retirement plan?

2. Would it be helpful to engage a retirement coach who can support you and hold you accountable to develop and act on a tailored plan to suit your life stage and needs?

3. What planning skills and experiences have you had that may help you as you contemplate and plan for your retirement years?

4. What plans have you developed in anticipation of your retirement?

5. What does a meaningful and fulfilling retirement look like to you specifically? How would you describe your ideal retirement day?

6. What core values do you want to guide your retirement decisions and daily choices?

7. How much of your identity is tied to your current work role, and how might this shift affect your sense of self in retirement?

8. What aspects of your working life do you want to carry forward into retirement, and what do you want to leave behind?

9. How will you handle the loss of workplace structure, colleagues, and professional status?

10. How will your relationships change in retirement, and what do you want to nurture?

11. What role do you want family, friends, and community to play in your retirement years?

12. How will you maintain social connections and build new ones outside of work?

13. How will you structure your days to maintain energy, purpose, and cognitive engagement?

14. What activities or practices will you prioritise to age well and maintain independence?

15. What new skills, knowledge areas or experiences do you want to pursue in retirement?

16. How do you want to contribute to others or society during your retirement years?

17. What unfinished dreams or interests from earlier in life do you want to revisit?

18. How do you want to structure your time and create rhythm in your retirement days?

19. Where do you want to live, and how might your living situation need to evolve?

CHAPTER THIRTEEN

IMPLEMENTING YOUR RETIREMENT PLAN

'The secret to getting ahead, is getting started.'

—Mark Twain

'To achieve great things, two things are needed: a plan and not quite enough time.'

—Leonard Bernstein

You have completed developing your plan, so, as Nike says, you 'just do it', right?

This is correct, but the word 'just' can be misleading. It suggests that implementing the plan is easy and quick. However, in most cases, it's not; it's more about hard work with a dose of resilience.

Research indicates that while 92% of people set goals or plans, only 8% achieve them. The difference is never about the quality of the plan; it has everything to do with the approach to its implementation.

If you find implementing your plan easy, that's fantastic! Execute your actions, achieve your goals, then set up your action plan for your next goal on your priority list.

However, as you work through each category towards a thriving retirement, you will inevitably face challenges. These may be external obstacles or internal resistance, such as procrastination.

It might happen as you implement your first action plan, or when you are working on your fourth goal. Either way, let's discuss how to maintain momentum as you act toward establishing a framework to thrive in retirement.

As previously discussed, change is challenging. It requires perseverance, discipline, tenacity, and determination. We might have good intentions, but intentions without commitment will inevitably lead to diminished motivation as initial enthusiasm fades. When we relapse and experience lethargy, it's time to reset and answer the questions: *'Why am I doing this in the first place?'* and *'What did I originally identify as the primary benefits of implementing the plan I created?'*

Here's an example of a client I supported who relapsed and was able to regroup and complete his plan:

Robert (62) worked with me to create a comprehensive plan for his upcoming retirement, which was three years away. His holistic plan encompassed four key areas:

- *Maintaining physical health through regular exercise and improved nutrition.*

- *Fostering meaningful social connections beyond work colleagues.*

- *Pursuing his dormant interest in woodworking.*

- *Transitioning work responsibilities to create more time for personal interests.*

Initially energised, Robert joined a gym, signed up for a woodworking class, and started meeting neighbours monthly for coffee.

The Relapse

After four months of progress, Robert's motivation began to wane. His gym membership lapsed. He dropped out of the woodworking class after missing several sessions. His social coffee meetings became sporadic, and he worked longer hours than ever. When I checked in with him six months later, Robert felt frustrated and said, 'I guess I am just meant to be a workaholic. I don't know how to do anything else.'

The Reset Strategy

I coached Robert to reset using these approaches:

- Normalise the setback: *I explained that transitioning from a work-centred identity is challenging, and setbacks are part of the process and should not be seen as personal failures.*

- Identify the barriers: *Together, we discovered that he felt guilty about leisure time activities. He felt overwhelmed, trying to build an entirely new lifestyle while still working full-time.*

- Start small and build gradually: *Instead of overhauling everything, we focused on taking a 15-minute daily walk during lunch breaks. He also set up one social interaction per week in his diary (whether a brief chat or attending a community event monthly). His wife, Sarah, became his accountability partner. At realistic intervals, she asked him how he was progressing with his initiatives.*

- Connect activities to existing routines: *Robert began listening to woodworking podcasts during his commute, making the interest feel more accessible without requiring separate time blocks.*

- Reframe the transition: *By adding more activities to his already busy life, I helped him reframe it as a gradual process of small, manageable steps. He shifted his focus to activities that would sustain him over the long term.*

- Create gentle accountability: *We agreed on bi-weekly text check-ins instead of formal meetings. Robert shared one thing he enjoyed outside of work that week.*

Within eight months, Robert naturally expanded his walking routine and reconnected with old friends. He also set up a small workshop in his garage because the changes felt organic, and he believed these small adjustments were motivating.

I have struggled for years to find an exercise routine that I enjoy and can stick to consistently, so it becomes part of who I am.

I love sports and have previously tried regular cycling. Still, I find it very difficult to establish a routine, especially during the week, given my long work hours, raising kids, and letting the weather decide whether I exercise or not. I've joined various gyms over the years, which I found very helpful, but I became bored within a year; the repetitive nature of gyms ultimately wore me down. I tried swimming in 50-meter pools and reached a good level of fitness, and I gained quite a bit of muscle; however, when we moved to a different suburb without a 50-meter pool, I relapsed.

We now reside on Sydney's Northern Beaches, and during COVID, working from home became a necessary routine for at least two years. During this period, I took up power walking along the stunning cliffs of this beautiful stretch of beaches. I began with a three-day schedule (Monday, Wednesday, and Friday). After six months, I increased it to five days (Monday to Friday) with golf on alternate Saturday mornings with local mates. Power walking has now become my 'Atomic Habit!'

Why have I been able to stick to this activity?

First, I thoroughly enjoy it, who wouldn't, when you have such beautiful scenery, whether it's clifftops, roaring waves crashing against the shore, or golf courses and lush green parks?

Second, when it rains, I jump on the exercise bike (so, no excuses not to exercise!).

Third, we acquired a Spoodle pup, Brandy, a year ago, and he requires frequent exercise. I find it helps reduce his natural proclivity to chew and destroy my dwindling supply of socks!

Of course, not everyone has access to coastal cliff walks. A client in Canberra found her rhythm with mall walking during harsh winters, while another in Melbourne enjoyed early morning walks around their local golf course.

The key is to discover what genuinely brings you joy while serving your health goals. Importantly, have a clear purpose, i.e., a simple answer to the question, *'Why am I doing this?'*

Stages of Change

In Chapter 2, we discussed in considerable detail how to manage change. You may find it helpful to revisit it to refresh your memory of the principles.

Any action plan you put into motion is likely to bring about a change, possibly a substantial one, to your current lifestyle and daily routine. Be gentle with yourself. Give yourself enough time for the change to take effect. Remember that asking for support shows wisdom.

Be familiar with the different stages. Recognise that relapse can be a natural part of creating permanent change. When we recalibrate, we can come back stronger and more determined. So, avoid beating yourself up when relapse comes knocking!

Implementation Roadblocks and Solutions

When it comes to changing your situation and implementing a beneficial solution, it is easy for the subconscious to find all manner of reasons not to execute the change.

No doubt some or all the examples below will resonate with you:

- Perfectionist paralysis: 'I will start when I have the perfect setup.'
- All-or-nothing thinking: 'I missed three days, so what's the point?'
- Social resistance: Family and friends questioning changes.

- Energy depletion: Taking on too much simultaneously.

- Identity confusion: 'All my life I have been a different person with old habits, so I am not likely to change at this late stage of my life.'

So, how many of these examples are you familiar with? If you said one or more applied, guess what, you are human! When you experience these feelings, avoid negative thoughts and replace them with positive ones.

Time To Celebrate

There is value in taking the time to acknowledge any successes you have achieved in implementing your retirement plan. Celebrating serves as encouragement and can help motivate you to continue to progress.

I worked with a client called Karen, who created a milestone celebration.

Karen, a 58-year-old hospital administrator, came to me feeling overwhelmed about her approaching retirement. She had the financial aspects in place, but felt lost about the 'life' part of retirement. Together, we developed a holistic plan that covered three key areas:

- *Rekindling her passion for watercolour painting.*

- *Building stronger community connections.*

- *Creating a structured volunteer role that would give her purpose.*

Six months into implementing her plan, Karen had made remarkable progress. She'd enrolled in a local art studio's advanced watercolour class. She joined the neighbourhood gardening club and began volunteering as a literacy tutor at the community centre twice a week.

She completed her first significant watercolour piece. A landscape of the lake where she planned to spend her mornings. She felt it was time to acknowledge how far she'd come!

Karen didn't want to celebrate alone or let the moment pass unmarked. Instead, she planned a small gathering. She invited her art class friends and the three children she tutored. She displayed her completed watercolour and created a small exhibit of photos (her first nervous day at art class, the community garden beds she'd helped plant, and photos of her reading with the children).

Karen recognised that her progress deserved acknowledgment, not just from herself but from the community she was building. She later told me that hearing others reflect on her growth made the changes feel real and sustainable.

Six months later, after fully implementing her retirement plan and leaving her hospital job, Karen hosted an even bigger celebration. She said she valued marking transitions with the people who mattered most to her journey.

This story illustrates how celebrating progress reinforces positive changes that will sustain you through your transition to retirement.

While Karen's approach worked well for her social style, celebration can take many forms. Some prefer quiet personal acknowledgments. For others, a special dinner, a meaningful purchase, or simply a journal entry to document progress. Others might prefer a celebration with the family.

These different types of celebration might not suit everyone. However, find what is personally meaningful and helps keep you on track. Make sure you recognise your achievements. It's also a lot of fun to do so!

Retirement Coach

We will discuss the benefits of a retirement coach in detail in the next chapter. In every coaching session, your retirement coach can be your ideal accountability partner and will (if they're well-qualified and proficient) bring extensive experience, supporting you 100% to create a path to a thriving retirement.

To bring it all together, it is helpful to utilise a system or process that will positively help you achieve and fully execute your plans.

The Progress Exercise

This exercise helps you create a support system that naturally drives you toward your retirement goals.

Step 1: Map Your Goal Landscape

Begin by listing your 3-5 primary non-financial retirement goals. For each goal, write it in the centre of a separate sheet of paper, then draw four quadrants around it labelled: Daily Habits, Weekly Rhythms, Monthly Checkpoints, and Support Network.

GOALS

DAILY HABITS	WEEKLY RHYTHMS
MONTHLY CHECKPOINTS	SUPPORT NETWORK

Step 2: Design Your Daily Habits Quadrant

For each goal, identify one small daily action that moves you forward. The key is to make it so simple that you cannot fail. If your goal is to maintain physical fitness, write 'exercise for twenty minutes and do five minutes of stretching before turning in'. These micro-habits create momentum without overwhelming your current routine.

Reflect on your personal energy patterns and lifestyle constraints. If you're naturally energetic in the mornings, establish your habits then. If you're caring for grandchildren three days a week, plan your routines around that schedule. If you have an apartment with a patio, think about focusing on both indoor and outdoor plants or indoor alternatives.

Step 3: Establish Weekly Rhythms

Create a weekly practice that complements your daily routine. Maybe a Saturday morning 30-minute walk for fitness, or a Wednesday evening art studio session for creativity. Weekly patterns provide structure and allow flexibility in how you pursue your goal.

Step 4: Create Monthly Checkpoints

Design a monthly review system that's both reflective and forward-looking. This is about recalibrating, where needed. Ask: 'What worked well this month?' 'What obstacles did I encounter?' 'What one minor adjustment would help next month?' Schedule this review on your calendar like any necessary appointment.

Step 5: Build Your Support Network

Identify specific people who will help sustain each goal. For a learning goal, you might list a friend as your accountability partner for book discussions, the local library book club for community engagement, and Professor Chen as the subject matter expert. Be specific about what type of support each person provides and remember to appreciate them.

Step 6: Design Environmental Triggers

Review your physical space and identify any changes that would make achieving your goals easier. If you want to cook more, place a cookbook on the kitchen counter. If you are learning photography, keep your camera visible near your keys. Your environment can be a motivating factor.

Step 7: Plan Your Celebration Markers

Finally, determine the best way to acknowledge your progress. Maybe completing your first month of daily walks earns you a new audiobook, or finishing a community education class means dinner at your favourite restaurant with your partner or friend. Planning celebrations makes them more likely to happen.

This exercise transforms vague retirement dreams into concrete, sustainable practices. Instead of relying on motivation, you create a system where progress occurs naturally through daily habits, weekly rhythms, monthly reflection, environmental design, and social support. When clients complete this exercise, they often say: *'I can see how this will work'.*

Once established, this system runs itself, allowing you to focus on your retirement purpose rather than constantly worrying about progress.

Reflection Questions for a Thriving Retirement

1. What is a small step you can take this week to progress one aspect of your plan?

2. Which part of your plan feels overwhelming? How can you simplify it?

3. What excuses do you keep using to delay implementation, and what's behind them?

4. Who can you share your specific goals with to create accountability?

5. If you could only accomplish three things in your first year of retirement, which areas would have the most significant impact on your satisfaction?

6. Which elements of your plan must occur before others?

7. What are you trying to do all at once that could be done more effectively one at a time?

8. Which aspects of your plan require the most lead time, and when should you start?

9. How will you measure progress on areas such as developing deeper relationships?

10. What signs will tell you that you are drifting away from your retirement purpose?

11. How often will you review and adjust your plan?

12. What is working better than expected, and how can you do more of it?

13. What support and resources do you need before you can move forward effectively?

14. What will you do when motivation wanes or when initial enthusiasm fades?

15. How will you maintain momentum during setbacks or when progress feels slow?

16. What daily or weekly routines can help you stay aligned with your retirement goals?

17. How can you transition your retirement activities into habits rather than intentions?

18. What environmental changes do you need to make to support your new lifestyle?

19. Which aspects of your plan need regular maintenance? What approach will work?

CHAPTER FOURTEEN

YOUR RETIREMENT COACH

'A coach supports you in moving from intention to commitment, which in turn leads to action.'

—Peter Cheel

'Coaching helps you to take responsibility for your life, let go of what others think and become your true self. It's about you creating the life that you want and deserve.'

—Emma-Louise Elsey

Research suggests that structured support, especially professionally facilitated interventions, can improve adjustment and well-being during significant life transitions such as retirement. Systematic reviews and recent studies indicate that such support helps mitigate adverse psychological effects and improves emotional adaptation compared with no structured support.

The retirement coaching profession is rapidly growing globally, with practitioners emerging across North America, Europe, Australia, and Asia. Although the profession may be relatively new in some regions, its principles and benefits remain universal.

In this chapter, we'll look at how you can receive the support that will help you build the vibrant retirement that you deserve. A retirement coach will support and facilitate you in conceiving and establishing your vision for retirement. They will guide you (as an individual or a couple) through the plans and practical implementation steps to turn your vision into a reality. They will also support your transition, ensuring you are ready to lead a purposeful, fulfilling life in this next stage.

Why a Retirement Coach?

Retirement is your final opportunity to shape your life intentionally. Naturally, you'll want to prepare thoroughly to make the most of this important stage.

It is likely to be a very significant change from everything you've done in your life so far. Therefore, it can be highly beneficial to have a retirement coach to help you view life and opportunities from fresh and different perspectives. Receiving an external perspective can help you uncover 'blind spots' about what retirement could look like. Having someone walk alongside you to challenge and stretch your thinking about this stage will help you identify insights you may not otherwise discover. On occasion, when I conclude a coaching session, I wonder whether it was worthwhile for the client. When I ask the client about the session, the most common response tends to be:

'Simply being able to talk this through with you and to process and ventilate ideas with you has been most helpful.' When you share what's on your mind, it can elevate or change your perspective, and the way forward often seems more straightforward.

Truth be told, it's not always easy to do what we already know we should do, particularly when we work alone.

I'm a huge advocate for having an accountability partner. Not everyone needs one if they are highly motivated, disciplined and excellent at self-leadership. However, in my experience, such individuals are relatively rare. As mentioned previously, only two out of ten people seek financial advice in their lifetime, and fewer plan for retirement intentionally. It's no surprise that having an accountability partner is uncommon, especially when it comes to retirement planning.

Another key reason is that you don't have to face it alone! Help is on hand.

Here is an example of a client I supported a few years ago, which illustrates the benefit of an accountability partner:

Susan, 59, is a hospital administrator who was planning to retire in 18 months. She was financially prepared but had no hobbies and few friendships outside of work, and she admitted she wouldn't know what to do with herself in retirement. She typically worked 60-plus-hour weeks for 25 years. She told me that she derived most of her identity and social connections from her work. Her situation isn't unusual. When we spend a third of our lives at work, it's natural that our work becomes central to who we are and how we connect with others.

In the initial coaching session, we concentrated on establishing an accountability framework. I spent time helping Susan recognise that, while being financially prepared is very important, so too is working through lifestyle preparation and all other related areas. By the end of the session, Susan committed to the following actions:

- *Try one new activity monthly, for six months.*

- *Nurture three non-work friendships.*

- *Establish boundaries for home and work time.*

- *Schedule monthly coaching check-ins to review progress.*

Initially, Susan started with passion and energy, but as work became busier, things began to slip. Susan repeatedly cancelled social plans and new activities. She was also reluctant to delegate responsibilities, fearing the organisation would struggle without her constant involvement.

As I became increasingly aware of her relapse, I introduced the following coaching intervention strategies:

• *Boundary Setting: I challenged Susan by asking her a rhetorical question about her cancellation of pottery class for the third time: 'What message are you sending yourself about the value of your future life in retirement?'*

• *Sense of Identity: We explored Susan's identity in great depth, beyond her job title, helping her identify values and interests that predated her career.*

• *Delegation Practice: Susan committed to leaving work by 6 p.m. twice a week. She also committed to conducting a position audit of her primary responsibilities. Once completed, she would delegate one responsibility each month for six months.*

• *Social Accountability: I asked Susan to text me photos from each new activity or social event she attended or participated in.*

The result of these undertakings?

Over the course of four months, Susan discovered a passion for painting. She reconnected with two college friends and joined a hiking group, successfully delegating her weekend hospital rounds. She told me that she was feeling less anxious about retirement and more excited about the possibilities.

The key accountability elements Susan committed to were:

• *Photo evidence of activity participation.*

• *Weekly work boundary check-ins.*

• *Confrontation about self-worth being tied to long work hours.*

• *Gradual delegation timeline with monthly milestones.*

This transformation occurred over 18 months of coaching. Susan later commented that, without external accountability, she would have continued the cycle of working excessive hours until her actual retirement. Her 'aha' moment was realising that it would have left her woefully unprepared for her transition to retirement.

This case study illustrates how accountability through coaching facilitates commitment and action. It enables clients to develop personal relationships and engage in meaningful activities essential for a fulfilling retirement.

I was honoured to meet the late Sir John Whitmore in 2007. He defined coaching as:

'Unlocking people's potential to maximise their performance. It's helping them to learn rather than teaching them.'

In his book, 'Toward a Coaching Psychology,' the late Dr Tony Grant defined coaching as:

'A solution-focused, result-oriented, systematic process in which the coach facilitates the enhancement of work performance and the coachee's self-directed learning and personal growth.'

You can readily identify the emphasis on accountability, where John refers to 'helping them to learn', and Tony refers to the 'coachee's self-directed learning.'

The following chart clarifies different types of coaching and shows the purpose and results of retirement coaching.

CATEGORY	PURPOSE	METHODOLOGY	OUTCOME
Business & Executive Coaching	Unlock an individual's inherent potential.	Asks questions to tap individuals' wisdom & facilitate solutions to problems & challenges, and, where relevant, utilise assessments.	Optimisation of the person's full potential.
Life Coaching	Offering advice on personal matters, such as career, health, and relationships, to help improve a client's quality of life.	Supports the client in defining their personal goals and subsequently coaches them to achieve them through a series of questions.	Clarity of direction and clarity about what's what will fulfil the person.
Retirement Coaching	Facilitate a person's transition to a flourishing and purposeful life in retirement.	Utilises specific tools and a retirement planning framework, augmented by open-ended coaching questions, and referral to specialists where applicable.	The person is ready to retire and has an established, executable plan that addresses all aspects of retirement.

CATEGORY	PURPOSE	METHODOLOGY	OUTCOME
Mentoring	Impart wisdom & knowledge from years of experience	Storytelling based on personal experience. Providing helpful advice in a range of different areas, often focused on developing leadership competencies.	Increased knowledge in dealing with work situations, interpersonal relationships, and people leadership.
Counselling	Career direction & support	Advocate, advise, support and guide the person.	Enhanced personal and or career clarity.
Therapy	Psychological healing and insight, as well as support with coping mechanisms.	Understand history, increase self-awareness, observation & behaviour change, and, where relevant, utilise assessments.	Insight into history, understanding of feelings, dysfunctional behaviour, shifts patterns. Increased self-awareness.
Training	Acquisition of specific skills & development	Targeted multi-dimensional learning experiences	Competency in a specific subject, skill or behaviour.

There are many different types of coaching, including business coaching, leadership development coaching, executive coaching, life coaching, and health coaching. A retirement coach specialises in retirement, focused specifically on helping you achieve your retirement goals.

Some of the broad benefits of engaging a retirement coach:

- Objective support to move from intention to commitment, action, and implementation.

- An outside, independent voice that will encourage and facilitate your reflection about your purpose for the future.

- Someone who can inspire you to develop effective retirement plans for immediate, medium, and long-term goals that cover all key areas.

- Holistic retirement planning, supported and held accountable by a coach, will facilitate a smooth transition to an active life that positively impacts the community, family, and self.

More specifically, a retirement coach can assist with:

- Clarity and Goal Setting: Helping you clarify your retirement goals, values, and priorities and encouraging you to set specific, achievable objectives.

- Emotional Preparation: Recognising that retirement can trigger a variety of feelings, including excitement, anxiety, and uncertainty, the retirement coach will support you in managing these emotions and offer coping strategies.

- Lifestyle Planning: Assisting you in creating a fulfilling and meaningful retirement lifestyle. Additionally, encouraging you to explore new hobbies, activities, volunteering opportunities, and other ways to stay active and maintain a sense of purpose.

- Health and Wellness: Facilitating discussions about maintaining physical and mental well-being during retirement. Additionally, encourage healthy lifestyle choices and help you develop strategies to stay active and maintain social connections.

- Transition Management: Helping you manage the practical aspects of retirement, including the timing of retirement, social security benefits, healthcare options, and other logistical considerations.

- Coping with Change: With significant changes to daily routines and social networks, retirement coaches will be supporting you in adapting to these changes and embracing new possibilities.

- Decision Making: Supporting you in making important decisions related to your retirement, such as relocation, downsizing, or pursuing new educational opportunities.

- Building Resilience: Helping you develop resilience and coping skills to handle challenges that may arise during retirement, such as adjustments to unexpected circumstances.

- Accountability and Support: Providing an external source of accountability and supporting you as you work toward your retirement goals.

- Family Dynamics: Facilitating discussions about retirement planning with your family members and helping you navigate potential conflicts or expectations.

Here are two case studies incorporating the specific benefits outlined:

Case Study 1

Patricia, 59, is a recently divorced high school principal facing retirement in six months. She's experiencing panic attacks about her future, has no retirement vision beyond not working, and her adult children are pressuring her to move closer to them across the country.

The coaching intervention:

- *Clarity and Goal Setting: I guided Patricia through a values exercise. She identified that independence, learning, and helping others are her core drivers. Together, we set specific goals: (establish a new routine within 90 days, explore three volunteer opportunities, and create a 5-year personal vision).*

- *Emotional Preparation: Patricia worked through her fears about loneliness and financial insecurity. I provided her with coping strategies for anxiety, including journaling and mindfulness techniques, helping her reframe retirement as freedom rather than loss.*

- *Lifestyle Planning: We explored Patricia's interest in literacy work, discovering local tutoring programs and community college teaching opportunities. I also helped her envision a retirement filled with learning and community contribution.*

- *Transition Management: I assisted Patricia in identifying her actual retirement date (aligned with the end of the school term) and in creating a transition timeline that included gradually reducing work commitments.*

- *Family Dynamics: Using role-playing, Patricia practised setting boundaries with her children about the pressure to relocate. Later, Patricia met with her family and presented her decision to remain in her house while maintaining close relationships with them.*

- *Coping with Change: When Patricia struggled with the loss of professional identity, I encouraged her to develop new routines and social connections through volunteer work and continuing education classes.*

- *Decision Making: Patricia faced a significant decision about relocating. I provided a decision-making framework to help her weigh the pros and cons objectively. This resulted in a decision based on what was most important to her in the future.*

Some of the results of the coaching intervention:

- *Patricia transitioned confidently into retirement and established herself as a volunteer literacy coordinator. She enrolled in art classes and maintained her independence while strengthening family relationships. Her anxiety decreased as she developed a clear sense of purpose.*

Patricia's experience reflects global patterns. From teachers in Toronto to business managers in London and medical professionals in Sydney, the loss of professional identity is a real personal challenge. That's why it is so beneficial to discuss this topic with a support person and take the time to process the change.

Case Study 2

Michael, 58, planned to work until he turned 65. However, his doctor warned him about his severe risk of having a heart attack. He made the tough but correct decision to consider early retirement. He was the primary breadwinner for his wife and teenage son. This made him feel overwhelmed by his health concerns. He also feared losing his identity as a successful sales manager.

The coaching intervention:

- *Health and Wellness: I collaborated with Michael to develop a comprehensive wellness plan that included stress management, exercise routines, and dietary adjustments. We explored how retirement could improve his health outcomes by reducing stress.*

- *Emotional Preparation: Michael processed his grief over his changed circumstances and his fears about his family's financial security. I provided emotional support and helped him develop strategies to cope well with the necessary adjustment.*

- *Building Resilience: When Michael's cardiologist recommended immediate retirement, I helped him adapt quickly to this unexpected change. We developed a contingency plan, and I encouraged him to maintain an optimistic outlook about alternative paths forward.*

- *Transition Management: I assisted Michael in navigating the logistics of early retirement, including researching disability benefits and continuing health insurance. We also created a gradual work-reduction plan that helped reduce stress while maintaining his income.*

- *Accountability and Support: Michael committed to weekly health check-ins, monthly financial reviews, and maintaining his exercise routine. I provided consistent support during this challenging transition period.*

- *Lifestyle Planning: As we continued to meet, I discovered Michael's passion for mentoring young salespeople. I helped him explore consulting opportunities that could provide purpose and supplementary income without the stress of full-time employment.*

- *Family Dynamics: I facilitated conversations between Michael and his wife regarding role changes, financial adjustments, and mutual support during his recovery and career transition.*

- *Coping with Change: Michael struggled with the loss of his high-energy sales career. To address this, I helped him redefine what success meant to him. This included developing new daily routines that incorporated health priorities and a different focus. It was vital for him to maintain his sense of achievement and contribution.*

Some of the results of the coaching intervention:

- *Michael successfully transitioned to part-time consulting work, which improved his cardiovascular health. He experienced fulfilment and meaning in mentoring opportunities. Meanwhile, his family adjusted well to these changes, benefiting from better communication and a more equitable distribution of responsibilities. He also built resilience skills that helped him cope with* persistent health challenges.

Michael's health-related early retirement scenario is common. It impacts about 40% of early retirees in developed countries, making adaptability and resilience key areas of focus in retirement coaching.

Both case studies demonstrate how retirement coaching addresses the complete spectrum of retirement challenges.

Selecting a retirement coach who is both well-credentialed and aligned with your values is naturally challenging. It's an important decision to get right, considering the very positive impact it may have on your next stage of life.

Here are some questions and pointers on how to choose the most suitable retirement coach to meet your needs.

Does the prospective coach have proper and rigorous coaching qualifications (not simply a weekend course)? As a guide, they will have, as a minimum, an undergraduate degree in psychology or human behaviour, together with substantial coaching experience.

Request the names of two referees and call them. A very revealing question to ask: *'If you were beginning your retirement planning now, would you engage them as your retirement coach?'* If their response is delayed or overly diplomatic, that should raise a red flag for you.

Arrange a 'meet and greet' to evaluate if you can work well with this person. It's understood that we don't gel with everyone we meet, so do your due diligence.

Ask them about their retirement-coaching methodology. Listen for words such as retirement coaching, goals, accountability, support, regular sessions, open-ended questioning techniques, active listening, and motivational interviewing.

If they are the kind of person who freely offers advice, they're probably more of a mentor or, at worst, someone more focused on selling than coaching.

If their approach is to ask lots of questions and help you reflect and make your own decisions, then they may be worth pursuing. Avoid people who provide you with a manual to complete.

An effective retirement coach will align their focus with your needs and aspirations. Avoid coaches who offer 'cookie-cutter' solutions.

The most comprehensive retirement coaching typically involves a minimum of six sessions, each lasting approximately 90 minutes to two hours.

Before you proceed, it is imperative to insist on a written agreement that includes mutual expectations.

If your coach applies rigour, you can be confident they will ask you many intelligent questions. They will probe and positively provoke you. They will aim to guide you in establishing the best executable plan. One that you have the confidence to implement. They will also support you on your implementation journey.

How do you Find a Retirement Coach?

Since coaching in Australia is largely unregulated, the quality of the relationship often matters more than a person's stated credentials. A good retirement coach helps you think through your own answers rather than prescribing solutions. Trust your instincts about whether someone truly listens and understands your unique situation.

Here are some areas to initially investigate and consider:

Specialist retirement transition programs

- Some universities and community education centres run retirement planning workshops that aren't about money. Facilitators of these programs often offer one-on-one coaching.

- Organisations like U3A (University of the Third Age) sometimes have connections to lifestyle coaches or run peer-led transition programs.

- Council-run community centres and neighbourhood houses occasionally host retirement lifestyle programs.

Professional networks and associations

- Career coaches who specialise in late-career transitions often expand into retirement lifestyle work. Review the Career Development Association of Australia (CDAA).

- Life coaches with specialisations in "third age" could be helpful places to start.

- Some corporate outplacement firms offer retirement transition coaching, particularly when an individual has left due to redundancy or an early retirement package.

Word of mouth and referrals

- Ask your financial planner if they know retirement coaches, they refer clients to (good planners recognise the non-financial aspects matter).

- Pre-retiree seminars and expos (RetireInvest and similar organisations sometimes include lifestyle components).

- LinkedIn searches for "retirement coach Australia" or "retirement transition coach". Review their content to see if they focus on lifestyle vs. finance.

Alternative angles

- Some corporate wellness coaches work with people transitioning out of long careers.

- Retirement villages and communities sometimes bring in lifestyle coaches for residents. Start with some of the larger Retirement Village companies and ask them who they use for such seminars.

- Books and podcasts by Australian retirement lifestyle coaches often mention their practices.

- Here is a link to a Directory of Retirement Coaches in Australia. Be aware that this list is by no means exhaustive. https://www.retirementoptions.com/Retirement_Coach_Directory.asp?Country=Australia

- Remember to also tap into your existing networks. I'm constantly amazed that when you need something or you are researching a particular topic there are always people out there who can refer you to the right people. So don't be afraid to ask; most people like to help others.

Red Flags When Selecting a Coach

- Coaches who guarantee specific outcomes. No one, regardless of their abilities, can make promises when outcomes depend on variables beyond their control.

- Those who push their own retirement vision rather than helping you discover yours. The actual value of a retirement coach lies in their ability to help you explore and establish your own unique retirement vision.

- Practitioners who seem more focused on selling additional services than coaching. Always be clear and assertive about what you are looking for in terms of support.

- Anyone who dismisses the emotional aspects of the retirement transition.

- Coaches who lack an understanding of the non-financial aspects of retirement planning.

The coach you ultimately choose should be qualified, experienced, and knowledgeable. They will be able to create a personalised approach that addresses your unique situation. Retirement coaching is an investment in your future and well-being. It can serve to enhance your retirement experience.

If you face a health challenge, you will want the best medical specialist suited to your needs. The specialist has significant qualifications, experience, and knowledge, and charges accordingly. Likewise, given that your retirement could reasonably last around thirty years, it would be prudent to invest in the best support your finances can provide.

Engaging a retirement coach is a wise decision. Preparing for this important stage can give you confidence that you'll be well-prepared to enjoy a thriving and meaningful life.

Reflection Questions for a Thriving Retirement

1. Have you ever engaged a leadership, business, or executive coach?

2. How do you think you could work with and benefit from engaging a retirement coach?

3. What research will be worthwhile to consider when choosing a retirement coach to support your plan for your retirement?

4. What specific aspects of retirement planning feel most overwhelming or unclear to you right now?

5. How comfortable are you with being vulnerable about your fears and dreams with a coach?

6. What would success look like to you after working with a retirement coach for six to twelve months?

7. What is your budget for retirement coaching?

8. Do you prefer working face-to-face, or are you comfortable with virtual coaching relationships?

9. How much time can you realistically commit to coaching sessions each month?

10. What coaching style would work best for your personality?

11. Do you need a coach who specialises in your situation (entrepreneur, executive, caregiver, single, etc.)?

12. What support systems do you have in place (spouse, family, friends) that could complement your work with a retirement coach and encourage you?

13. What barriers (geographic, financial, cultural, or personal) might prevent you from accessing retirement coaching?

14. If coaching isn't accessible, what alternative support systems could you develop?

CHAPTER FIFTEEN

FINAL WORDS FROM SOME WISE PEOPLE

'It's not the young man who should be considered fortunate, but the old man who has lived well, because the young man in his prime wanders much by chance, vacillating in his beliefs, while the old man has docked in his harbour, having safeguarded his true happiness.'

—Epicurus

After exploring the practical aspects of retirement planning throughout this book, we turn to the wisdom of people who have lived the longest retirement of all! People in their 90s and beyond can offer a unique perspective on what truly matters over decades of post-career life.

I have had the privilege and honour of interviewing some nonagenarians (plus), hearing their wisdom on how to lead a whole and flourishing long life.

These conversations took place between 2024 and 2026 and were conducted as informal interviews, focused on sustaining life satisfaction and offering practical tips. While each person's experience is unique, common themes emerged that align with research on successful aging and life satisfaction.

Jason: (Age 103 in 2024) – He passed away in late 2024

Jason represents the 'reluctant retiree', someone whose retirement was driven by practical necessity rather than careful planning. Yet he experienced fulfilment through adaptation and community connection.

He had three sons and a daughter. He lost his wife over twenty years ago. He spent a long and successful career in public service as an Engineer. Upon retiring at age 65, he emigrated to Australia with his wife (his children were already living there). At age 66, he returned to the workforce full-time, working for his son's building and construction company.

I asked what had driven him to return to full-time work at age 66 after retiring. His simple response: *'I needed the money!'* Later, he transitioned to working three days per week, then two. He ultimately stopped working in his 80s. He said he stopped not because he was tired or had had enough of work; instead, he was sick of driving in Sydney traffic!

He never planned for his retirement, but he knew when it was time. He wanted to spend more quality time with his family, play bowls, and enjoy watching sports. He had a mobile phone, which he used to watch sports when not using his TV. He enjoyed the aspects of life that he hadn't been able to enjoy when he worked.

He was never one to sit around relaxing. He played bowls twice a week and did the crossword every day. When his wife was alive, they went on day trips and met with friends (four couples) once a week. He also walked 12 km every day with a friend and attended his local synagogue once a week. He was highly engaged in his community and in life.

He said to me: *'You must adjust as you age, you become restricted, and you must be flexible and realistic about your own limitations'.* In his late 90s, he watched a lot of TV (mainly documentaries, sports, and politics). He also continued to read the Torah.

He said his philosophy on life was 'always to do the CAN CAN, which is:

- Do as much as you can
- Whatever you wcan
- As well as you can
- To whoever you can
- For as long as you can

What a wonderful philosophy for a life well-lived. I discovered later that this inspiring set of principles was originally attributed to English Anglican pastor, theologian and evangelist, John Wesley:

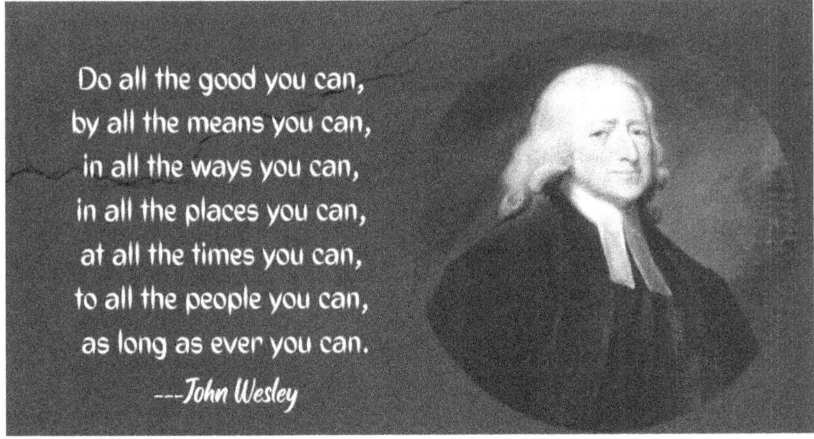

This philosophy translates across cultures and languages. Whether expressed as the Japanese concept of 'ikigai' (life purpose), the Danish 'hygge' (contentment), or the Australian 'fair dinkum' (authenticity), the principle remains: engage fully with life!

He also added some other words of wisdom:

'You need consistency in life' or, as he put it, the *'handrails of life.'*

According to Jason, the primary handrails are family, friends and religion. These handrails sustained him in a rapidly changing world.

He said, *'In life, you need a good support team. An experienced mountaineer can't climb Mt. Everest without Sherpas, and a tight-knit family is that support.'*

He said, tongue in cheek, that you must choose the right parents because *'it's all in the genes.'* As you can no doubt notice, he had a sharp wit and a wonderful sense of humour.

The values he inherited from his parents were honesty, truthfulness, loyalty and friendship. He lived his life abiding by these values, which undoubtedly served him well.

He said you need to take care of yourself. Exercise regularly, maintain a healthy diet, and stay positive (a good sense of humour is an excellent antidote to illness). Also, keep your mind active. It's also about being a bit lucky!

He suggested that people continue working for as long as they can and remain active by pursuing a variety of hobbies and interests.

Concluding, he said, *'don't fight off the ageing process. Don't be too introspective. Stay positive.'*

He previously played cricket, rugby, and tennis. During the interview, he said he now watches it. He was registered with Stan Sport and Foxtel. He also loved music and had registered with Spotify at the age of 102!

What an inspirational person.

Bridget: (Age: 90 in 2026)

Bridget was born in Sydney to Irish immigrant parents and was the youngest of four children.

All three siblings lived well into their nineties, and her grandmother reached 103, so it seems Bridget inherited good genes!

Growing up in the family home was quite tough for Bridget. Her parents were very strict and followed a set of rules. They taught her the values of integrity, respect, and the importance of family.

Bridget was never academically focused at school; her passion was sports. She excelled at athletics, swimming, and diving, representing her school successfully in all three. She won the all-schools diving championships. She also enjoyed softball, which she kept playing after leaving school, and she represented NSW at a state level.

She undertook secretarial studies after finishing her schooling and then worked in the timber industry. Later, she was employed as a flight attendant for East West Airlines, operating regional routes.

She met her first husband at a bush dance, and as newlyweds, they settled in a regional town before building their own home on Sydney's North Shore. It was during these years that she developed a love for friends and community. Their house was in a cul-de-sac, which made it easy and enjoyable to get together for street parties and gatherings. They formed a very close-knit community, and one proof of that was their weekly trip to the local beach for a swim and picnic during summer. The friendships they built lasted for decades.

Bridget had two children with her first husband, and she now has two grandchildren whom she adores and spends quality time with whenever the opportunity presents itself.

As a single mother raising two children, she had to secure full-time employment. She spent several years working at a school and later in retail. She also worked at a charity shop, where she met her second husband, who was volunteering there at the time.

I asked her to assess her level of satisfaction in certain areas of her life, such as interests, hobbies, philanthropy, sports, family, spirituality, and friends. When I asked her to rate her satisfaction and sense of meaning with her friends, her reaction was palpable. Her whole face lit up, and she had a beaming smile. I mentioned that friends appeared to be vital to her. She replied: *'Oh yes, my friends are very important to me; very important.'*

Regarding spirituality, she mentioned that her Christian faith provided her with meaning and purpose in life. It served as her anchor and compass and was one of the reasons she volunteered to work in the prison ministry at Silverwater. She wanted to support people in need.

Bridget never planned a specific time to retire. Her husband was older than her, and when he retired, she wanted to spend quality time with him. She said she just knew that was the right time and the right thing to do.

Living alone after her husband passed, she realised that she needed to get out of the house, and that's exactly what she does every day. She's up early each morning, slipping into her 'swimmers' and in the water at their local beach before 7.30 am for laps in the ocean pool. She swims with a group of friends; they call themselves the 'buckets'. Initially, she swam with two friends, and this small group has now grown to 25. After the swim, she and some of her friends head to the local café for coffee and a chat!

Her life is very full: visiting friends, watching documentaries and health videos, listening to podcasts, going to church, meeting with her connect group, or attending a lecture at her local Probus group.

When I asked her about any disappointments in retirement, she looked at me blankly, paused and then said: *'I really can't think of any.'*

She said that what has sustained her in retirement are her deep friendships, her faith, exercise, and socialising with people of all ages. She said she draws energy from her friends and people in general. They lift her up and encourage her.

When I asked her what advice she would give to anyone considering retirement, she responded: *'Look after your health by eating well and exercising regularly. Get out and mix with people, spend less time at home. Participate in hobbies that interest you and that you enjoy. Be engaged in social groups, be outward-looking, and, importantly, be thankful.'*

As we were concluding the interview, she mentioned that she had recently completed an AI (artificial intelligence) course and was eager to learn more about it! Since then, she downloaded the ChatGPT app to her phone and enjoys researching different topics.

Bridget embraces life and lives it to the fullest – what an inspiration she is!

Bill: (Age: 104 in 2025)

Bill was born in India to Missionary parents and emigrated to Australia at a very young age. He worked in clinical medicine, specifically in hospital-based clinical research.

His wife battled with mental health, and this contributed to their separation. His second marriage led to a new career as a social welfare officer (specialising in drugs and alcohol). At age 56, he and his wife relocated to Darwin, Northern Territory, to take on a community consulting role. At age 64, he retired and returned to Canberra.

However, he soon came out of retirement to assume the role of consultant at what was then known as CRS (Commonwealth Rehabilitation Services). Later, he became Director at the Ethics Institute and then Commissioner of the National Health and Medical Research Council... so much for retirement!

Some words of wisdom from him:

- He has a range of interests. Family, friends and relationships are vital to him. He shows a strong sense of curiosity about the world and everything in it. He is fascinated by what makes people tick. Cosmology and Psychology interest him. He has always been an optimistic person and sees opportunities in most circumstances.

- He wasn't ambitious, even though he excelled in his career. He stumbled upon opportunities but has always valued helping people. His purpose is to be available, to listen to and support others. He sees himself as an other-centred person.

- He said curiosity and having options have sustained him throughout his life.

- In retirement, he emphasised the importance of developing interests that will endure and outlast one's frailty.

- He said it's worth living well, laughing much and leaving this world better than you found it.

- One of his hobbies in retirement is writing haikus.

This haiku is a brilliant description of what life is and what it can be during those twilight years:

Is your glass half empty or half full? Mine, I like to think, is emptying and filling at the same time, even into old age, and that it will be full to the brim, perhaps overflowing, when I die. For those who prefer a different imagery, it can be represented on graph paper as two diverging lines. One line, the emptying, runs downwards over time, failing eyesight, getting deaf, heart trouble, hip problems, loss of memory, cancer and 101 other 'going down the hill' things we hear about so commonly. I'm getting old, falling apart. I'm not what I used to be. Regrets for what's past.

The other line climbs upwards over time. Often ignored and overlooked. Here, there is hope for the future: becoming someone new. A mixture of cumulative experience, thank goodness for living longer and increasing maturity. Seeing more and more sights that delight; hearing more and more inspiring music; being thrilled by TV sports and dramas and travel documentaries; less self-consciousness; more contentedness in being 'just as I am', authentic 'me'; enjoying relief from onerous responsibilities of bringing up a family, especially in the complexities of this day and age, and being a productive worker. Appreciating the smiles and hellos and help that come more frequently from utter strangers, even from young damsels, to a harmless-looking old man!; the increased opportunity to explore, albeit superficially,

   AN ABUNDANT LIFE BEYOND RETIREMENT

interests beyond those that were all-consuming in one's earlier life; getting my life, the world, and the mysteries of life itself into better perspective – or so I think!; and so on.

The downhill stuff, the emptying of the glass, is very real and natural. Something to be deplored but accepted and adjusted to. So, too, with the inevitable gradual reduced capacity of the glass itself. It is the inflow and fullness that can give satisfaction, a sense of well-being, despite the shrinkage, and infirmities, disease and even dementia.

My hope is that any attention to these decrements will be minimal, diluted and submerged by the upfilling of my little glass right up to the time when I topple off my perch. A fare-thee-well (not ill) departure.

This little haiku provides a realistic, yet optimistic view of aging:

Declining … Yet ascending … Contentedly

These two remarkable reflections capture what gerontologists call the paradox of aging. The simultaneous decline and growth that characterise successful later life. His imagery of diverging lines offers a framework for understanding how losses and gains can coexist.

I close with an excellent quote from Bill:

'I have lived my whole life learning how to live. As a slow learner, I need a very long life. My studentship is by no means finished.'

James: (Age: 95 in 2025)

James demonstrates how an international perspective and diverse interests can enrich retirement, notably by maintaining strong community connections.

James said that at a very young age, his parents instilled in him the values of fairness, integrity, and doing the right thing.

He was born in Zimbabwe (then known as Rhodesia) and, after completing his schooling, studied medicine, qualifying as a GP before pursuing further medical studies. At a young age, he took over his father's business and became an effective business operator.

In his early to mid-adult years, he developed a real passion for music, whether playing the piano, listening to records (he has over 8,000), or attending concerts. He was actively involved in the community, serving as a councillor for 23 years and as mayor for one year.

He is interested in languages, and in addition to English, he speaks French, German, and Italian.

Learning to speak French may have influenced his love for cooking, as he taught himself to cook 'Cordon Bleu!'

Philanthropy was a focus and interest. He also served on the Cancer Council, Blood Transfusion Board, and Chamber of Commerce.

He believes in the benefits of exercise, and at 95, he still goes to the gym. He previously played a lot of tennis and enjoyed long-distance running, having completed 16 marathons, including one unsuccessful attempt.

Although he never married, family remains very important to him, and he often gets together with different families. He said he was brought up in the Jewish faith but is now a 'born-again heathen'! No doubt you're beginning to appreciate his dry sense of wit.

He has three close friends who live in London, New York and Johannesburg. He used to visit them regularly during his travel days.

He said he contemplated retiring after selling his business at age 70. He built a nest egg in Jersey before settling in Rose Bay, Sydney, at 83. His purpose in retirement is to keep going as long as possible.

When he settled into retirement, he said he spent his week going to the gym, jogging, practising languages, and playing bridge with men from his old school (who lived in Sydney). He plays bridge three times a week and has amassed winnings of $3,000 to date.

When asked what has given him the greatest satisfaction and joy in retirement, he replied without hesitation: *'Keep keeping on, gym, bridge, working at a classical radio station, continuing to drive and brain training exercises in the evening.'*

Reflecting on disappointments in retirement, he said: *'COVID, as it prevented me from travelling.'* Recently, he has had to stop jogging outside, but still goes for gentle runs indoors.

When asked what sustains him and continues to fill his cup, he paused and then said, *'People do not realise their self-worth. I have always had a strong and healthy self-belief.'*

I asked him what advice he would give to anyone thinking about retirement. His response: *'Keep active (particularly exercise), keep moving, stimulate your brain, be pragmatic and positive and embrace all life has to offer.'*

What wise, sage advice from someone who is nearing centenarian status!

His advice reflects research findings on regions where people live the longest and healthiest. The common factors he mentions (physical activity, mental stimulation, social connection, positive outlook) appear consistently in longevity studies worldwide.

Despite their different careers, public service engineering, retail, medical research, and business, these four people share remarkable similarities:

- Each adjusted expectations and activities as circumstances changed.
- All prioritised relationships and contributions to others.
- Curiosity and mental engagement remained central throughout their life.
- Each maintained exercise routines that were adapted to their capabilities.
- Whether through family, service, or mentoring, each found purpose in contributing to something greater than themselves.

These patterns align with findings from longevity research across diverse populations, including Okinawan centenarians, Sardinian shepherds, and American blue zone* communities (*locations such as Loma Linda, California and Nicoya, Costa Rica).

This little poem must be many years old, and therefore, the language is not necessarily contemporary. Nevertheless, I have included it, as it sums up what a good life could look like for all of us!

That man is a success
Who has lived well,
laughed often and loved much:
Who has gained the respect
of intelligent men and the love of children.
Who has filled his niche
and accomplished his task.
Who leaves the world better than he found it.
Who has never lacked appreciation of earth's beauty,
or failed to express it
Who looked for the best in others
and gave the best he had.

—Waldo Emerson

A Little Perspective

These four short accounts come from individuals who have lived (and in the case of three of them, continue to live) exceptionally long and healthy lives. While their wisdom holds value, it is essential to recognise that many factors contributing to longevity (genetics, access to healthcare, well-being, socioeconomic stability, and luck) are not entirely within a person's control. Their advice should be considered alongside the understanding that successful ageing takes many forms, and shorter lives can be just as meaningful and well-lived.

Each story, hopefully, serves to inspire you to reflect on your own values, priorities, and possibilities. Notice which aspects resonate most strongly with you. Those reactions often indicate areas worth exploring further in your own retirement planning.

As you close this book and begin creating your retirement plan, carry with you both the practical frameworks from earlier chapters and the wisdom of those who have walked this path before you. Your retirement will be uniquely yours, but seeking others' advice can help enrich it. Build on a foundation of both wisdom and evidence-based planning.

The aim is to craft your own version of a fulfilling life. May your retirement be enriched with the adaptability of Jason, the curiosity of Bill, the engagement of James and the vitality and positivity of Bridget. Remember that the best retirement planning blends practical preparation with an openness to life's ongoing surprises.

Reflection Questions for a Thriving Retirement

1. What caught your eye and made you think when you read their stories?

2. What aspects of their example of living a good life would you like to emulate?

3. If you were to adopt one or more of their ideas, what would you need to start or stop doing?

4. Which of their core values or life principles resonates most strongly with you, and why?

5. How do their perspectives on what matters differ from what you prioritise in your life?

6. What surprised you most about their mindset toward ageing, loss, or life's challenges?

7. What did you notice about how they maintained purpose in different life stages?

8. What daily habits, routines, or mindsets contributed to their longevity and life satisfaction?

9.   How did they navigate major life transitions, and what can you learn from their resilience?

10. If you could have a conversation with them, what would you want to ask them?

11. What would you need to change in your life to adopt their approach to living well?

12. How do these stories challenge typical assumptions about what is achievable as people age?

EPILOGUE

The four remarkable people we met in the previous chapter lived out the principles captured in the following poem.

Measure of a Man

And this is the measure of the man –
Not how did he die? But how did he live?
Not what did he gain? But what did he give?
These are the units of a man, as a man,
To measure the worth, regardless of birth.
Not what was his station. But had he a heart?
And how did he play his eternal part?
Was he ever ready, with a word of good cheer?
To bring back a smile, to banish a tear?
Not what was his church? Nor what was his creed?
But had he defended those really in need?
Not what did the sketch in the newspaper say?
But how many were sorry when he passed away?
—Anon.

Naturally, the words in this poem are equally important for everyone, not just men!

As you prepare for your own retirement transition, this poem provokes the more profound questions:

- What kind of person do you want to be in retirement?
- How will you experience fun, joy and laughter?
- What legacy will you leave in the hearts of those whose lives you touch?

If you choose, you can use this poem as practical inspiration and a guide for your retirement planning. The questions it poses can inform decisions in your retirement plan:

- How will you maintain the energy to 'bring back a smile, to banish a tear'?
- Who will be 'sorry when you pass away' because of the difference you made?
- How will you 'defend those really in need'?
- What 'word of good cheer' will you be known for?

These are practical ways to assess whether your retirement plan supports not only your comfort but, more importantly, your character, the core of what makes you unique.

And so, your journey begins!

Your journey may very well be the most intentional phase of your life. You now have the frameworks, tools, and wisdom to create a retirement that honours your practical needs, preferences and your core values.

The conceptual planning phase is complete when you finish this book. The living phase begins with your very next decision. Whether that involves scheduling your first retirement coaching session, having that conversation with your spouse or close friend, taking that health assessment, or simply asking yourself, *'What kind of person do I want to be in retirement?'*

You have a treasured opportunity to start a flourishing future now.

In years to come, may your life be measured not by what you accumulated, but by what you contributed, not by the comfort of your retirement, but by the character you displayed throughout it.

Your legacy is a story still to be written!

PART IV

YOUR SUPPORT SERVICES AND RESOURCES

In this section, I have provided extra information and referral websites to assist you. Some of the information will be more relevant to certain people than others, so be discerning about what will be most helpful for you.

If you're not already signed up to the MYGOV website, it's worth doing so since the Retirement section provides lots of helpful information. https://my.gov.au/en/services/ageing/retirement/planning-your-retirement

Government Benefits and Support Services

There are a range of benefits that you may qualify for when you retire, (which will more than likely be covered in the MYGOV website) i.e.:

- Health discounts such as dental, optometry, prescriptions and GP bulk billing

- Energy discounts and rebates

- Concessions on council rates

- Water rebates

- Transport discounts

- Vehicle registration and driver's license concessions

- Discounts for fitness and recreational activities.

- Aged Pension

National Seniors Australia

https://nationalseniors.com.au/news/latest-in-finance/what-government-financial-benefits-could-you-be-entitled-toquestion

A range of benefits, payments and services are explained and outlined on the Department of Social Services website (click on the tab 'Older Australians'): https://www.dss.gov.au/seniors/related-agencies-sites

It's worth highlighting the following information on this website.

Australian government agencies

- Australian Taxation Office
  General tax information including details regarding offsets
  for senior Australians and pensioners.

- Department of Human Services
  The Department of Human Services provides support in
  retirement with a range of payments including Age Pension,
  Pension Loans Scheme, Pension Bonus Scheme and Seniors
  Concession Allowance.

- Department of Veterans' Affairs
  Information about pensions, health, housing and
  commemorations for veterans and their families.

- Department of Health
  Information on government health programs, including
  information on ageing and aged care.

- Department of Employment
  Provides national leadership in education and workplace
  training, transition to work, and conditions and values in the
  workplace.

- Attorney-General's Department
  Information on protecting the rights of older Australians,
  including elder abuse.

Resources for seniors

- National Information Centre on Retirement Investments
  (website unavailable)
  Free, independent, confidential service which aims to improve
  the level and quality of investment information provided to
  people with modest savings who are investing for retirement or
  facing redundancy.

- My Aged Care
  Australian Government's online source of information for
  Australians over 50.

- Age Discrimination
  Information from the Australian Human Rights Commission.

- Advisory Panel on the Economic Potential of Senior Australians
  Information from the Secretariat.

- Experience Pays – Jobactive
  Provides information about the Restart program and the
  benefits of employing mature-age workers.

- Elder Abuse (link is external)
  Compass – A national knowledge hub and online resource
  dedicated to providing information on issues of elder abuse.

- My Aged Care Government website, outlining support for
  financially disadvantaged Australians: www.myagedcare.gov.au/
  support-financially-disadvantaged-people

- Payments and services for people retiring or accessing aged
  care. Help for people who care for older Australians. Services
  Australia: www.servicesaustralia.gov.au/ageing

Volunteering

https://govolunteer.com.au/seniors-aged-care-volunteering

https://www.volunteeringaustralia.org/#/

Australian Business Volunteers: https://www.abv.org.au/

https://www.volunteeringvictoria.org.au/

https://www.australianvolunteers.com/

https://www.dfat.gov.au/people-to-people/australian-volunteers-
program

https://www.volunteerworld.com/en/volunteer-abroad/australia

https://www.gooverseas.com/volunteer-abroad

https://probonoaustralia.com.au/volunteer/

https://www.volunteeringwa.org.au/#/

https://www.gviaustralia.com.au/volunteer

https://www.volunteerhq.org/

University of the Third Age

https://www.sydneyu3a.org/

Medical Support

https://www.eldercare.net.au/

https://retirementessentials.com.au/health-card/

https://www.servicesaustralia.gov.au/health-care-and-ageing?context=60057

https://www.agedcareguide.com.au/information/benefits-and-entitlements-for-retirees-and-seniors

https://www.health.gov.au/health-topics/aged-care

https://www.digitalhealth.gov.au

https://www.dva.gov.au/health-and-treatment/veteran-healthcare-cards/commonwealth-seniors-health-card

https://creakyjoints.org.au/government-pensions-benefits-services-people-chronic-health-issues/

https://www.healthdirect.gov.au/help-to-remain-living-at-home-if-you-have-a-chronic-disease-or-serious-illness

https://integratedliving.org.au/services/help-at-home?

Financial Support

https://reversemortgagesydney.com.au

https://www.myagedcare.gov.au/support-financially-disadvantaged

https://www.servicesaustralia.gov.au/most-viewed-payments-for-retirement

https://www.servicesaustralia.gov.au/financial-services-when-thinking-about-retirement

https://www.dss.gov.au/about-the-department/benefits-payments

https://www.aihw.gov.au/reports/australias-welfare/age-pension

https://www.nsw.gov.au/life-events/retirement/what-to-do-when-youve-retired/sorting-out-your-finances

https://www.disabilitygateway.gov.au/income-finance/financial-support/sa

https://www.aph.gov.au/About_Parliament/Parliamentary_
Departments/Parliamentary_Library/pubs/BriefingBook46p/
RetirementIncomes

https://www.qld.gov.au/seniors/legal-finance-concessions/
financial-advice-support

https://www.industrysuper.com/retirement-info/retirement-age/
the-big-question/

Well–Being

https://www.dss.gov.au/communities-and-vulnerable-people-
programs-services/seniors-connected-program

https://www.gcma.net.au/health

https://www.healthdirect.gov.au/older-people-and-mental-health

https://www.australianretirementtrust.com.au/learn/education-
hub/mental-health-at-retirement

https://nutritionaustralia.org/division/nsw/senior-mental-health-
tips/

https://coronavirus.beyondblue.org.au/I'm-supporting-others/
older-people/supporting-older-people-during-COVID-19

https://www.visionaustralia.org/services/find-services/seniors/
support-wellbeing

https://www.nsw.gov.au/life-events/retirement/what-to-do-
when-youve-retired/mental-health-and-legal-support/mental-
health-services

Hobbies and Interests

https://www.irt.org.au/the-good-life/fun-things-to-do-in-
retirement/

https://sixtyandme.com/20-serious-and-fun-things-you-can-do-
in-retirement/

https://www.aboutover50.com.au/hobbies-other.html

https://www.challenger.com.au/personal/retirement/be-
retirement-ready/a-guide-to-a-confident-retirement

https://www.agedcareguide.com.au/information/finding-purpose-in-your-retirement

https://mensline.org.au/mens-mental-health/adjusting-to-retirement/

https://www.arcadiawaters.com.au/5-great-retirement-hobbies-that-are-great-for-your-health-wellbeing

More information

- Money Smart, an Australian Securities and Investments Commission website, has free and impartial financial guidance and tools to help you secure your financial future.

- Seniors Enquiry Line, delivered by UnitingCare Community, provides information on concessions, social activities, household assistance, retirement accommodation, financial and legal matters, health, education, transport, etc.

- Queensland Government services and information covers various topics of interest to seniors.

- Your Rights at Retirement guide, produced by the Australian Human Rights Commission, covers topics, including health, aged care, wills and end-of-life decisions.

- Financial Planning Association of Australia provides a list of authorised financial planners in your area.

- Association of Independent Retirees is a not-for-profit volunteer organisation for fully or partly self-funded retirees.

- The Smart Traveller website has information for seniors about preparing for their trip, staying healthy, and getting help overseas.

Financial Retirement Planning Books

The recommended top 20 books:

Benz, C. (2024). *How to retire: 20 lessons for a happy, successful, and wealthy retirement*. Wiley.

Birken, E. G. (2022). *The 5 years before you retire: Retirement planning when you need it the most* (2nd ed.). Adams Media.

Collins, J. L. (2016). *The simple path to wealth: Your road map to financial independence and a rich, free life*. JL Collins LLC.

Kiyosaki, R. T., & Lechter, S. L. (1997). *Rich dad poor dad: What the rich teach their kids about money that the poor and middle class do not!* Plata Publishing.

Moon, B. K. (2022). *The ultimate retirement planning guide: Achieve financial freedom and live a fulfilling life.* Independently published.

Olen, H., & Pollack, H. N. (2016). *The index card: Why personal finance doesn't have to be complicated*. Portfolio.

Orman, S. (2020). *The ultimate retirement guide for 50+: Winning strategies to make your money last a lifetime.* Hay House.

Pfau, W. D. (2021). *Retirement planning guidebook: Navigating the important decisions for retirement success.* Retirement Researcher Media.

Piper, M. (2021). *Can I retire? How much money you need to retire and how to manage your retirement savings, explained in 100 pages or less* (2nd ed.). Simple Subjects, LLC.

Ramsey, D. (2003). *The total money makeover: A proven plan for financial fitness*. Thomas Nelson.

Richards, R. (2019). *Passive income, aggressive retirement: The secret to freedom, flexibility, and financial independence (& how to get started!).* Independently published.

Sethi, R. (2019). *I will teach you to be rich: No guilt. No excuses. No BS. Just a 6-week program that works (2nd ed.).* Workman Publishing.

Smith, J., & Sirianni, J. (2021). *Budgeting for retirement: How to plan for a comfortable future.* Independently published.

Snow, T. D. (2020). *Retirement planning QuickStart guide: The simplified beginner's guide to building wealth, creating long-term financial security, and preparing for life after work.* ClydeBank Media LLC.

Swedroe, L. E., & Grogan, K. (2019). *Your complete guide to a successful and secure retirement.* Harriman House.

Vettese, F. (2018). *Retirement income for life: Getting more without saving more.* ECW Press.

Wheeler, D. (2020). *The essential retirement guide: A contrarian's perspective.* Wiley.

Zelinski, E. (2004). *How to retire happy, wild, and free: Retirement wisdom that you won't get from your financial advisor.* Visions International Publishing.

Zweig, J. (2003). *Your money and your brain: How the new science of neuroeconomics can help make you rich.* Simon & Schuster.

Bogle, J. C. (1999). *Common sense on mutual funds: New imperatives for the intelligent investor.* Wiley.

General Retirement Planning

The Simple Path to Wealth – JL Collins
Focuses on passive investing, financial independence, and wealth-building strategies.

The Bogleheads' Guide to Retirement Planning – Taylor Larimore, Mel Lindauer, et al.
Based on the principles of Vanguard founder John Bogle, it emphasises index investing and practical retirement strategies.

How to Make Your Money Last: The Indispensable Retirement Guide
– Jane Bryant Quinn
A guide on managing retirement savings for longevity, covering Social Security, annuities, and investments.

Investing & Wealth Management for Retirement

The New Retirementality – Mitch Anthony
Encourages a mindset shift from traditional retirement views and focuses on purposeful wealth management.

The 5 Years Before You Retire – Emily Guy Birken
A step-by-step guide to preparing for retirement in the final crucial years.

Your Money or Your Life – Vicki Robin & Joe Dominguez
A classic on financial independence and aligning money with life goals, useful for early retirement planning.

Tax and Withdrawal Strategies

Retirement Planning Guidebook – Wade Pfau
A comprehensive deep dive into retirement income planning, Social Security, and risk management.

The Bucket Plan – Jason L. Smith
A structured approach to managing retirement savings and reducing risk through strategic withdrawals.

Tax-Free Retirement – Patrick Kelly
Focuses on tax-efficient strategies using insurance and other tools to maximize retirement savings.

Retirement Made Simple – Noel Whittaker
Offers clear guidance on retirement funding, housing, and lifestyle choices, helping Australians navigate the complexities of retirement planning.

How to Have an Epic Retirement – Bec Wilson
Provides insights into modern retirement, guiding readers through systems and valuable lessons to plan a fulfilling and financially secure retirement.

The Golden Years: How to Plan a Happy and Financially Secure Retirement - Jamie Nemtsas and Drew Meredith

Strategies for achieving a joyful and financially stable retirement, tailored to the Australian context.

Retirement Income for Life: Solving the Longevity Equation - David Orford, Peter Rowe, and Jim Hennington

A guide for financial planners to empower clients in managing longevity risk with lifetime income strategies.

Financial Advisors

https://www.superguide.com.au/retirement-planning/truly-independent-financial-advisers-in-australia

Financial Advice Association Australia (FAAA)

https://faaa.au/

Age pension

https://www.humanservices.gov.au/individuals/services/centrelink/age-pension

Withdrawing Super

https://www.ato.gov.au/Individuals/Super/Withdrawing-and-using-your-super/

Taxation on Super

https://www.ato.gov.au/Individuals/Seniors-and-retirees/Super/Taxation-of-super-benefits/

Concessions for retirees

https://www.nsw.gov.au/services/services-by-need/older-people/concessions/

Assessing your current assets and liabilities and future requirements

How much will you need?

https://www.superguide.com.au/retirement-planning/
comfortable-retirement-how-much-super-need

https://www.industrysuper.com/retirement-info/retirement-
calculators/retirement-needs-calculator/

https://www.moneysmart.gov.au/superannuation-and-
retirement/how-super-works/super-contributions/how-much-is-
enough

https://www.intheblack.com/articles/2019/08/01/how-much-
super-do-you-need

Tax in Retirement

https://www.ato.gov.au/individuals/seniors-and-retirees/retiring/

LIST OF REFERENCES

Borzykowski, B. (14 August 2013) Can Retirement Kill You? Retrieved from https://www.bbc.com/worklife/article/20130813-the-dark-side-of-the-golden-years

Daniels, A. C. (1994). Bringing out the best in people: How to apply the astonishing power of positive reinforcement. McGraw-Hill.

Baker, J. (1982). Tolstoy's bicycle: Being an amazing compendium of human history in which all mortal achievement is grouped by age from birth to death. St. Martin's Press.

Scott, S., & Day, L. (2021, July 25). Australians are living longer but what does it take to reach 100 years old? ABC News. https://www.abc.net.au/news/2021-07-25/longevity-ageing-centenarian-lifespan-life-expectency/100123434.

Australian Bureau of Statistics. (2024, November 8). Life expectancy, 2021–2023. https://www.abs.gov.au/statistics/people/population/life-expectancy/latest-release

Buchholz, K. (2021, February 5). Is 100 the new 80? Centenarians are becoming more common. https://www.weforum.org/stories/2020/07/is-100-the-new-80-centenarians-are-becoming-more-common/

Statista https://www.statista.com/chart/18826/number-of-hundred-year-olds-centenarians-worldwide/

Schaeffer, K. (2024, January 9). *U.S. centenarian population is projected to quadruple over the next 30 years*. Pew Research Centre. https://www.pewresearch.org/short-reads/2024/01/09/us-centenarian-population-is-projected-to-quadruple-over-the-next-30-years/

Vanguard. (2021, February 5). Life expectancy for retirees aged 65 years for both genders using Vanguard calculations from the Human Mortality Database. Vanguard. https://corporate.vanguard.com/content/dam/

corp/research/pdf/Planning-for-health-care-costs-in-retirement-US-ISGPLHC_072021_Online.pdf

Wilson, T., & Temple, J. (2022). New population projections for Australia and the states and territories, with a particular focus on population ageing. *CEPAR Working Paper 2022/11*. https://cepar.edu.au/publications/working-papers/new-population-projections-australia-and-states-and-territories-particular-focus-population-ageing

Buettner, D. (2005, November). The secrets of the world's longest-lived people. National Geographic, 208(5), 48–65.

Amenabar, T. (2023, January 25). Want to live to be 100? Here's what experts recommend. The Washington Post. https://www.washingtonpost.com/wellness/2023/01/25/centenarian-longevity-tips/

Statista Research Department. (2023). Share of the population who hold a bachelor's level degree or above in Australia from 1989 to 2023 [Graph]. Statista. https://www.statista.com/statistics/612854/australia-population-with-university-degree/

Australian Bureau of Statistics. (2024, November 20). Education and work, Australia, May 2024 (Catalogue No. 6227.0). https://www.abs.gov.au/statistics/people/education/education-and-work-australia/latest-release

Heraclitus. (2001). Heraclitus: Fragments (T. M. Robinson, Trans.). University of Toronto Press.

Kanter, R. M. (2012, September 25). Ten reasons people resist change. Harvard Business Review. https://hbr.org/2012/09/ten-reasons-people-resist-change

Greene, J., & Grant, A. (2001). Coach yourself: It's your life, what are you going to do with it? Momentum Press.

Rosten, L. (1978). Passions & prejudices: Or some of my best friends are people. McGraw-Hill.

Smith, A. (1967). The faith of Helen Keller: The life of a great woman. Harper & Row.

Greater Good Science Centre. (n.d.). Purpose definition | What is purpose. https://greatergood.berkeley.edu/topic/purpose/definition

Newman, K. M. (2020, July 14). How purpose changes across your lifetime. Greater Good Science Centre. https://greatergood.berkeley.edu/article/item/how_purpose_changes_across_your_lifetime

Burrow, A. L., Sumner, R., & Netter, M. (2014). Purpose in adolescence. ACT for Youth, 1–4. https://www.actforyouth.net/resources/rf/rf_purpose_1014.pdf

Calvo, E., & Sarkisian, N. (2006). Does working longer make people healthier and happier? Centre for Retirement Research at Boston College. https://crr.bc.edu/wp-content/uploads/2006/02/wob_2.pdf

Kim, E. S., Kawachi, I., Chen, Y., & Kubzansky, L. D. (2017). Association between purpose in life and objective measures of physical function in older adults. JAMA Internal Medicine, 177(8), 1148–1155. https://doi.org/10.1001/jamainternmed.2017.2415

Hill, P. L. (n.d.). Purpose, Aging, Transitions, and Health (PATH) lab. Washington University in St. Louis. https://psych.wustl.edu/purpose-aging-transitions-and-health-lab-patrick-hill

Kim, E. S., Sun, J. K., Park, N., Kubzansky, L. D., & Peterson, C. (2013). Purpose in life and reduced risk of myocardial infarction among older U.S. adults with coronary heart disease: A two-year follow-up. Journal of Behavioural Medicine, 36(2), 124–133. https://doi.org/10.1007/s10865-012-9406-4

Nelson, J. (1961). Wisdom for our time. Harper & Row.

Cambridge University Press. (n.d.). Well-being. In Cambridge English Dictionary. https://dictionary.cambridge.org/us/dictionary/english/well-being

Cherry, K. (2019, January 22). What is well-being? Definition, types, and well-being skills. Psychology Today. https://www.psychologytoday.com/us/blog/click-here-for-happiness/201901/what-is-well-being-definition-types-and-well-being-skills

Borzykowski, B. (2013, August 14). Retirement raises depression risk—But a glass of wine may help. BBC Capital. https://www.bbc.com/capital/story/20130814-retirement-raises-depression-risk-but-a-glass-of-wine-may-help

McCrindle Research Pty Ltd. (2022). The changing faith landscape of Australia. https://mccrindle.com.au/app/uploads/reports/The-changing-faith-landscape-of-Australia-Report-2022.pdf

Canadian Mental Health Association. (n.d.). What's your stress index? https://cmha.ca/find-info/mental-health/check-in-on-your-mental-health/whats-your-stress-index/

O'Donnell, M. P. (2009). Definition of health promotion 2.0: Embracing passion, enhancing motivation, recognising dynamic balance, and creating opportunities. American Journal of Health Promotion, 24(1), iv-iv. https://doi.org/10.4278/ajhp.24.1.iv

American Psychological Association. (n.d.). Resilience. In APA Dictionary of Psychology. https://dictionary.apa.org/resilience

Covey, S. R. (1989). The 7 habits of highly effective people: Powerful lessons in personal change. Free Press.

Merriam-Webster. (n.d.). Health. In Merriam-Webster.com dictionary. https://www.merriam-webster.com/dictionary/health

Oxford University Press. (n.d.). Health. In Oxford Reference. https://www.oxfordreference.com/view/10.1093/oi/authority.20110803095735856

Cambridge University Press. (n.d.). Health. In Cambridge Dictionary. https://dictionary.cambridge.org/dictionary/english/health

Wikipedia contributors. (n.d.). Health. Wikipedia, The Free Encyclopedia. Retrieved February 16, 2025, from https://en.wikipedia.org/wiki/Health

Sahlgren, G. (2013). Work longer, live healthier: The relationship between economic activity, health, and government policy. Institute of Economic Affairs. https://iea.org.uk/publications/research/work-longer-live-healthier-the-relationship-between-economic-activity-health-and-government-policy/

Swenor, M. E. (2020, May 12). Stressed? 10 ways to lower your cortisol levels. Henry Ford Health. https://www.henryford.com/blog/2020/05/how-to-lower-your-cortisol-levels

Mayo Clinic Staff. (n.d.). How to reduce adrenaline production naturally: 9 tips. Mayo Clinic. https://www.mayoclinic.org/healthy-lifestyle/stress-management/expert-answers/how-to-reduce-adrenaline-production-naturally/faq-20431456

Ukiomogbe, J., & Ullman, S. (2022, June 24). 12 proven ways to raise serotonin levels and boost your mood. Healthline. https://www.healthline.com/health/ways-to-boost-serotonin

Mental Health America. (n.d.). What is noradrenaline? Mental Health America. https://mhanational.org/what-noradrenaline

Cleveland Clinic. (n.d.). Endorphins: What they are and how to boost them. Cleveland Clinic. https://my.clevelandclinic.org/health/body/23040-endorphins

Australian Bureau of Statistics. (2022). Leading underlying causes of death by sex in Australia (2022). National Mortality Database. https://www.abs.gov.au/statistics/health/causes-death/national-mortality-database/latest-release

NutritionFacts.org. (n.d.). 10 best ways to increase dopamine levels naturally. NutritionFacts.org. https://nutritionfacts.org/10-best-ways-to-increase-dopamine-levels-naturally/

Ukiomogbe, J., & Ullman, S. (2021, August 4). 6 ways to increase GABA naturally for anxiety without benzos. Healthline. https://www.healthline.com/health/ways-to-increase-gaba-naturally

Ukiomogbe, J., & Ullman, S. (2018, September 25). 12 ways to boost oxytocin naturally. Healthline. https://www.healthline.com/health/how-to-increase-oxytocin

National Institute on Aging. (n.d.). Cognitive health and older adults. National Institute on Aging. https://www.nia.nih.gov/health/brain-health/cognitive-health-and-older-adults

Neal, Joseph C. *Charcoal Sketches*. Philadelphia: T.B. Peterson, 1847.

Clark, F. H. (n.d.). *We've put more effort into helping folks reach old age than into helping them enjoy it*. AZQuotes. Retrieved from https://www.azquotes.com/quote/532640

Holland, T. (2015, December 7). *10 of the best home-swap and home-sharing websites.* The Guardian. https://www.theguardian.com/travel/2015/dec/07/10-best-home-swap-home-sharing-websites

U.S. Government. (n.d.). Visa waiver program and ESTA. USA.gov. Retrieved [date], from https://www.usa.gov/visa-waiver-esta

The Grey Nomads. (n.d.). The Grey Nomads – Travel & Adventure for Over 50s. Retrieved [date], from https://www.thegreynomads.com.au/

Mackey, M. (2012, April 23). What's the secret to a highly effective life? AARP. https://www.aarp.org/entertainment/books/info-04-2012/stephen-covey-highly-effective-life.html

QSuper. (n.d.). Creating a flexible retirement. She's on Q. Retrieved [date], from https://qsuper.qld.gov.au/shesonq/articles/retirement/flexible-retirement

Society for Human Resource Management. (2019). 2019 Employee Benefits: The evolution of benefits [Survey report]. SHRM. https://www.shrm.org/hr-today/trends-and-forecasting/research-and-surveys/pages/2019-employee-benefits.aspx

U.S. Census Bureau. (2019). American Community Survey 2014-2018 5-Year Data Release. https://www.census.gov/newsroom/press-kits/2019/acs-5-year.html

Picchi, A. (2019, December 19). More Americans are working into old age. MoneyWatch, CBS News. https://www.cbsnews.com/news/more-americans-are-working-into-old-age/

Organisation for Economic Co-operation and Development. (2023, December). Improving opportunities and working conditions for older workers can bolster pension system sustainability and address labour market shortages. https://www.oecd.org/en/about/news/press-releases/2023/12/improving-opportunities-and-working-conditions-for-older-workers-can-bolster-pension-system-sustainability-and-address-labour-market-shortages.html

Australian Human Rights Commission. (2018). Employing older workers. https://humanrights.gov.au/our-work/age-discrimination/publications/employing-older-workers-2018

McCrindle. (2017). Supply and demand; Australia as an ageing nation. https://mccrindle.com.au/article/topic/demographics/supply-and-demand-australia-as-an-ageing-nation/

Senior Community Services. (n.d.). Five benefits of volunteering in retirement. https://seniorcommunity.org/five-benefits-volunteering-retirement/

Yeung, J. W. K., Zhang, Z., & Kim, T. Y. (2018). Volunteering and health benefits in general adults: Cumulative effects and forms. BMC Public Health, 18, 8. https://doi.org/10.1186/s12889-017-4561-8

Tomioka, K., Kurumatani, N., & Hosoi, H. (2016). Relationship of having hobbies and a purpose in life with mortality, activities of daily living, and instrumental activities of daily living among community-dwelling elderly adults. Journal of Epidemiology, 26(9), 497–505. https://doi.org/10.2188/jea.JE20150079

Robson, D. (2025, January 13). How to live better in 2025: the power of giving. The Guardian. https://www.theguardian.com/society/2025/jan/13/how-to-live-better-in-2025-the-power-of-giving

Hattori, H., Hattori, C., Hokao, C., Mizushima, K., & Mase, T. (2019). Hobbies, are they really that important? The Centre for Cognitive Health. https://www.tcch.org/hobbies-are-they-really-that-important/

Snaedal, J., Palsson, S., & Arngrimsson, R. (2011). A controlled study on the cognitive and psychological effects of colouring and drawing in mild Alzheimer's disease patients. Geriatrics & Gerontology International, 11(4), 431–437. https://doi.org/10.1111/j.1447-0594.2011.00698.x

National Institute on Aging. (n.d.). Participating in activities you enjoy as you age. https://www.nia.nih.gov/health/healthy-aging/participating-activities-you-enjoy-you-age

Pillay, S. (2017, August 29). How hobbies impact your head and your heart. Psychology Today. https://www.psychologytoday.com/articles/how-hobbies-impact-your-head-and-your-heart

Bowie, D. (2013, September 25). David Bowie: The Rolling Stone interview. Rolling Stone. https://www.rollingstone.com/music/music-news/david-bowie-the-rolling-stone-interview-248073/

Encyclopedia Britannica. (n.d.). *Friendship*. Britannica. https://www.britannica.com

Cambridge University Press. (n.d.). *Family*. In *Cambridge Dictionary*. Retrieved 15 March 2022 from https://dictionary.cambridge.org/dictionary/english/family

Williams, P. (1974). [Song title]. On Here comes inspiration [Album]. A&M Records.

Degges-White, S. (2015, March 23). The 13 essential traits of good friends. Psychology Today. https://www.psychologytoday.com

Palahniuk, C. (2003). Diary. Doubleday.

Blue Zones Project. https://bakersfield.bluezonesproject.com/

Green, S. (n.d.). Legacy of love. Charisma Magazine. Retrieved 2 January 2021, from https://mycharisma.com/blogs/greenelines/legacy-of-love/ (Billy Graham quote)

Franklin, B. (n.d.). If you would not be forgotten as soon as you are dead, either write something worth reading or do something worth writing. [Attributed quote].

Oxford University Press. (n.d.). Legacy. In Oxford English Dictionary (Online edition). Retrieved [date], from https://www.oed.com

Merriam-Webster, Inc. (n.d.). Legacy. In Merriam-Webster.com dictionary. Retrieved 6 February 2023, from https://www.merriam-webster.com

Kerridge, I. (2022, July 2). Losing a parent changes not just us, but our whole world. Weekend Australian

StoryCorps. (n.d.). StoryCorps: Share your story. Retrieved 10 June 2023, from https://storycorps.org

Storyworth. (n.d.). Storyworth: Record your life story. Retrieved 10 June 2023, from https://welcome.storyworth.com

Memlife. (n.d.). Memlife: Record your story and turn it into a book. Retrieved 10 June 2023], from https://memlife.com/home

Legacy Stories. (n.d.). Legacy Stories: Preserve and share your legacy. Retrieved 10 June 2023 from https://legacystories.org

Gibran, K. (1923). The prophet. Alfred A. Knopf.

Kübler-Ross, E. (1969). On death and dying. Macmillan.

The New International Bible. (2011). Luke 12:25-26. Zondervan.

Leoni, J. (2016, February 28). Life well lived. Retrieved 203 November 2024 from https://www.julieleoni.com/blog/endings/life-well-lived/

Cobb, D. (2022). *2022 Wills and Estate Planning Study*. Caring.com. https://www.caring.com

Tilse, C., Wilson, J., White, B., Rosenman, L., & Feeney, R. (2015). *Having the last word* (ARC Linkage Project). University of Queensland.

Tilse, C., Wilson, J., White, B., Rosenman, L., & Feeney, R. (2015). *Having the last word* (ARC Linkage Project). University of Queensland. https://nmsw.uq.edu.au/project/families-and-generational-asset-transfers-making-and-challenging-wills-contemporary-australia

Australian Securities and Investments Commission. (n.d.). *Money Smart*. https://moneysmart.gov.au

UnitingCare Community. (n.d.). *Seniors Enquiry Line*. https://seniorsenquiryline.com.au

Queensland Government. (n.d.). *Services and information for seniors*. https://www.qld.gov.au/seniors

Queensland Human Rights Commission. (n.d.). *Protecting human rights in Queensland*. https://www.qhrc.qld.gov.au

Australian Human Rights Commission. (n.d.). *Your rights at retirement guide*. https://humanrights.gov.au

Financial Planning Association of Australia. (n.d.). *Find a financial planner*. https://fpa.com.au

Association of Independent Retirees. (n.d.). *Supporting self-funded retirees*. https://independentretirees.com.au

Australian Government. (n.d.). *Smart Traveller: Senior travel advice*. https://www.smartraveller.gov.au

Grant, A. M. (2001). *Toward a coaching psychology: Theory, practice, and research*. Australian Psychological Society.

Epicurus. (2005). *The art of happiness* (G. Strodach, Trans.). Penguin Classics.

"Do all the good you can." (n.d.). [Commonly attributed to John Wesley].

Whitmore, J. (2009). *Coaching for performance: Growing human potential and purpose* (4th ed.). Nicholas Brealey Publishing.

Finder. (2022, October). Financial advice statistics. Finder. https://www.finder.com.au/financial-advice-statistics

Gratton, L., & Scott, A. (2016**).** *The 100-year life: Living and working in an age of longevity.* Bloomsbury.

Mackay, H. (2013). *The good life: What makes a life worth living?* Macmillan.

Attributed to Emerson, R. W. (n.d.). *That man is a success* [Quote].

Anonymous. (n.d.). *And this is the measure of the man* [Poem].

Pryor, R. G. L., & Bright, J. E. H. (2005). *The Luck Readiness Index*. Retrieved from https://www.brightandassociates.com.au/luckreadiness.html

Robson, D. (2025, January 13). *How to live better in 2025: The power of giving*. The Guardian.

McGinley, P. (n.d.). A hobby a day keeps the doldrums away. [Quote].

Shaw, G. B. (n.d.). We don't stop playing because we grow old; we grow old because we stop playing. [Quote].

Stanley, E. (n.d.). Those who think they have no time for bodily exercise will sooner or later have to find time for illness. [Quote].

Stanley, E. (n.d.). Those who think they have no time for bodily exercise will sooner or later have to find time for illness. [Quote].

The Gerontologist. Interventions that support major life transitions in older adulthood: a systematic review. Cited National Library of Medicine.

Gill Livingston, Jonathan Huntley etal. (July 31, 2024) Dementia prevention, intervention, and care: 2024 report of the Lancet standing Commission.

ACKNOWLEDGMENTS

There are many people to thank for their roles in bringing this book to fruition. I recognise my parents' role in raising me, affording me an excellent education, and instilling in me a love for the English language.

The genesis of this book began with many discussions with three people: Jenny Kahn, a former work colleague and, later, with a good friend, Phil Pogson, about a Retirement Support Strategy for business and public-sector employees. This later morphed into writing this book!

Thanks to Book Coach and Editor Kylie Zeal, your patience (with all my ongoing questions), professionalism, and sage advice inspired me to finish the book. You challenged and encouraged me through the 'doldrums' and the frustrations. Also, thank you to Designer Julia Kouris and Typesetter Michelle Pirovich for your calmness, professionalism, and creativity. David 'Macca' Macdonald, who generously gave his time to proofread the book, your incisiveness and attention to detail greatly improved the manuscript! To my Professional Supervisor, who, during a session when I felt demotivated, positively challenged me after he asked, *'Why are you writing this book?'*

To my family, Clair, Thomas, and Chloe, thank you for your encouragement and patience when all you heard about was retirement planning! To my siblings, Margaret and Alan, my extended family, and my close friends, thank you for your encouragement and wise counsel.

ABOUT THE AUTHOR

Peter's life journey began in his birthplace, Cape Town, then took him through the UK and Europe, before settling in Australia, where he now resides on the Northern Beaches of Sydney.

He holds an undergraduate degree in Psychology and a Master's in Coaching Psychology from The University of Sydney. His career has spanned multiple executive roles, including Human Resources Director positions at global corporations and Regional CEO of a global not-for-profit organisation.

Drawing on this extensive corporate experience, Peter founded two coaching practices, Coaching2Lead and Business Coach Sydney, where he specialises in leadership, executive, business, and retirement coaching. He works with clients on leadership development, strategic planning, team alignment, and business growth. He also dedicates time to coaching and mentoring pastors from various Christian denominations and final-year students at his alma mater.

Peter maintains an active lifestyle that includes bodysurfing, sailing, kayaking, bushwalking, golf, travel, and photography. He is also actively involved in his local church in Avalon. His diverse background and commitment to personal growth have equipped him to be a trusted guide for those seeking a fulfilling and meaningful retirement.